Life, Death, and Beyond

D1258487

Mack Lyon

Publishing Designs, Inc.
Huntsville, Alabama

Publishing Designs, Inc.
P. O. Box 3241
Huntsville, Alabama 35810

Printed in the United States of America

ISBN 0-929540-17-4

To the memory of my dear mother,
Inez Lyon
who, in spite of severe adversity and
opposition, encouraged and supported me
in my preaching. Early in my ministry she
gave me a plaque by which she continues
to inspire me, long after her ability to
speak, and her death:

Only one life
'Twill soon be past
Only what's done
For Christ will last.

Contents

Foreword

The most productive part of the life of Moses was the last of three forty-year periods. His forty years in Egypt and forty years in the wilderness prepared him for his final forty years as God's leaders and great Lawgiver. Likewise the most effective work done by Mack Lyon has been in the last decade and in his mature years. His education, his radio and television experience in several places, and his mission successes both at home and abroad helped shape him into one of the most powerful television evangelists among us. The international television program, *In Search of the Lord's Way*, has wide acceptance both in and out of the church. In my judgment, it is the best television presentation of the gospel in the brotherhood.

Currently at least one gospel message a week is made available to 135 million American families in all fifty states on fifty television stations, eighty community cable systems, fifteen radio stations, and three satellite networks. It is rated in the top ten religious programs in America. At the request of viewers more than 110 thousand printed copies and audio cassette tapes of programs were mailed out in 1993.

It is also televised in Belize, Central America, and Kiev, Ukraine, as well as on many other stations throughout Russia, Ukraine, and Eastern Europe. It is broadcast via radio to the East African English-speaking nations of Kenya, Uganda, Tanzania, Zambia, and Malawi.

During the 1989-1990 season, it was broadcast by the United States Department of Defense via The Armed Forces Radio and Television Service to a one and a half million U. S. military families and a "shadow audience" of forty million people in seventy-five foreign nations and more that five hundred ships at sea. It was one of only three religious programs chosen for telecast on AFRTS during that season.

Bible messages he has so effectively proclaimed over television have been well received. They have dealt with serious problems of humankind and by using the Scripture he has given hope to the distraught and uninformed. Basic to all of his preaching is the preaching of the Bible which is God's power (Romans 1:16). As he preaches, he exudes kindness, humility and live, but at the same time, firm commitment to sound doctrine. Always he comes across to his audience as being believable. He speaks "the truth in love" (Ephesians 4:15).

Because so many of his lessons have been so helpful to television audiences, it is fitting that many of them should be collected into a book for further study. Mack Lyon has therefore prepared another volume: *Life, Death, and Beyond.* Since it deals with current national concerns and the ways people are hurting, it will have a ready acceptance.

With understanding, kindness, and civility he presents the Bible truth on questions on the hearts of millions. With amazing skill he gives answers to longing hearts who want to know about suicide, abortion, purpose of living, suffering, euthanasia, and life after death. It is a book of hope and not despair. Adult and young adult Bible classes will find it a profitable guide for study.

Likely Mack Lyon could not be accomplishing what he is doing without the broad experience in preaching in Oklahoma, Arizona, Texas, New Jersey, Australia, Singapore, Pakistan, Ceylon, and India. Also, he conducted radio and television programs in several cities. This background contributed to his present phenomenal success on television. Not all good preachers are good television and radio preachers, but Mack Lyon has mastered the art. Additionally, he has wielded an effective pen by clear writing of books and tracts. In 1966 he published the book, *Continuing Instant in Prayer* and in 1993, *Did You Miss the Rapture?*

Mack Lyon attended Freed-Hardeman College (now University). He graduated from the University of Oklahoma. He has done graduate study in counseling at East Central State University in Ada, Oklahoma.

He has ascended to the group of those who are most influential and he did so in his latter years. In the next decade his usefulness and influence will multiply to the glory of God and the spread of New Testament Christianity. We esteem him "very highly in love" for his "work's sake" (1 Thessalonians 5:13).

Dr. E. Claude Gardner
President Emeritus
Freed-Hardeman University
Henderson, Tennessee 38340

Editor's Preface

The material presented in *Life, Death, and Beyond* was developed for television and delivered by its author in the late 1980s and early 1990s. The speaker's script was so refined and exact that almost no editing was required. However, those procedures necessary for transferring spoken messages to the printed page so they can best be understood by the reader are set forth here for the careful student.

Though current events presented herein have already slipped into the pages of history, they have been left intact because they give spontaneity to the messages and will spark the interest of thousands of readers for many years to come.

Pronouns having reference to deity and not quoted from other sources are capitalized: He, His, Him, and Himself. Also, Heaven and Hell, when used as specifice after-life places, are capitalized as are the intermediate places of Tartarus, Hades, and the supposed place of Purgatory.

All quoted materials, including archaic spellings, are produced as in their original text with the following exceptions:

(1)   Capital letters that begin Bible verses have been changed to lowercase when they do not begin sentences or begin complete statement quotations.

(2)   Words or phrases emphasized by the author are italicized without any further indication that the emphases are his.

(3)   Author's comments, when interspersed with quoted material, are set off in brackets with no further explanation.

With great joy and much enthusiasm, we place this book in the hands of curious seekers and sincere students of God's word. May God's blessings rest with the earnest reader!

James B. Andrews

Preface

It is my strong conviction that you and I came into this world, not because we chose or when we chose, but because God had need of us. Therefore, there is a divine purpose for our being here at this precise moment in human history. Whether we have been a success when it is all over will not depend on the possessions or position or power we acquire or achieve, but whether we have accomplished that purpose for which we were born.

Some modern sage has observed that there are a few people in the world who make things happen; some watch what happens, but most of us simply ask, "What happened?" While we may find a bit of humor in that, it is sad, too, because so many good people seem to be just drifting along through life without the slightest idea why they are here. There is a great need to help people find meaning and purpose in life.

With the advent of modern medical science and technology have come some very difficult moral and ethical questions relating to life, death, and dying. Questions about the sanctity of life, when life begins, a person's right to take his own life, or the life of another when living becomes unbearable, are real questions. Regrettably, some of us have avoided teaching on these subjects leaving them to be answered by unbelievers. It is time to speak up. Consequently, human life has become cheap, the social order has collapsed, and violence threatens the lives of all our citizens.

Some of the earliest known writings, worship forms, and burial rites confirm mankind's universal desire to live on after death. Some pollsters have found that in the last decade people have shown more interest in the question of life after death than any other—even the national economy or debt. In the same time more than a thousand books have been published on the subject, most of them from the unbeliever's point of view. Many of us have stood around the grave about to receive the remains of a loved one or friend and rolled it over in our minds, "Is this the end, or is there something beyond this—more to come? If so, what? And where? Many people need help with this question from the Christian perspective.

Questions from our television audiences, people of every denominational background, reveal more than mere curiosity in the whereabouts of their dead loved ones. They would like to know all they can about what that deceased spouse or child or parent is doing. Are the dead conscious? We've tried to help with Bible teaching, but we are aware of the controversial nature of these subjects. If, in eternity, something should not be precisely as I have said, I promise I won't be found arguing with God because He didn't do it as I thought it would surely be.

We've addressed these questions of life and death and what lies beyond in our television and radio programs, *In Search of the Lord's Way.* They have drawn *tremendous* audience response. Many viewers requested they be published in book form. That is the reason for this publication.

All I know about any of it is what I have gleaned from living, from studies of the Scriptures and from what others have said and written. I have given credit for quotes where I could. Yet, I know my credits are incomplete. When I'm listening to someone on my car radio or in person, I often quickly jot down a thought which I consider personally helpful. Later, sometimes much later, when I sit down to insert the sentence in a message, I have no record of whose quote it is, or whether it is a quote or a paraphrase. I know that's being a bit careless, but had I known I would be publishing the material, I might have been more careful. So there is no possible way I can retrace my thinking to determine what I knew and when and from whom

I learned it. Dear reader, if I quoted you without credit, please forgive me and write me so I may make the revision in the next printing.

These messages are sent forth in this form, as they were delivered on television, with the prayer that some soul may find meaning for his life in this world and hope for life in the world to come.

Mack Lyon

1

Life,
Its Meaning

Psalm 8

O Lord, our Lord, how excellent is thy name in all the earth! who hast set thy glory above the heavens. Out of the mouth of babes and sucklings hast thou ordained strength because of thine enemies, that thou mightest still the enemy and the avenger. When I consider thy heavens, the work of thy fingers, the moon and the stars, which thou hast ordained; what is man, that thou art mindful of him? and the son of man, that thou visitest him? For thou hast made him a little lower than the angels, and hast crowned him with glory and honor. Thou madest him to have dominion over the works of thy hands; thou hast put all things under his feet: all sheep and oxen, yea, and the beasts of the field; the fowl of the air, and the fish of the sea, and whatsoever passeth through the paths of the seas. O Lord our Lord, how excellent is thy name in all the earth!

What is life? Who are we? What are we doing here? Is life really worth living? Quite obviously, people look at these questions from many different vantage points and arrive at very different conclusions. If we consult the dictionary for a definition of life, it will tell us that it's "the period from birth to death."

From a purely biological point of view, "life is an organismic state characterized by the capacity for metabolism, growth, reaction to stimuli, and reproduction." Materialism says that "the highest values or objectives of life lie in material well-being and pleasure and in the furtherance of material progress."

Hedonism says that "pleasure is the sole or chief good in life." Humanism says, "We can discover no divine purpose or providence for the human species." The noted infidel of the century past, Robert Ingersol said, "Life is a narrow vale between the cold and barren peaks of two eternities. We strive in vain," he said, "to look beyond the heights. We cry aloud, and the only answer is the echo of our wailing cry." The agnostic, Clarence Darrow, in his debate with Dr. Frederick Starr on the question, "Is Life Worth Living," defined life as "an unpleasant interruption of nothing, and the best thing that can be said of it is that it does not last long."

All of that is terribly dispiriting, don't you think? Such a dim view of life is totally devastating to many people and, without doubt, is the cause of much of the tragedy in our present society. You can easily see why a person who holds such a view might commit suicide, or choose to abort her little helpless, innocent preborn baby, or terminate the life of an elderly, disabled, unproductive parent, or commit many of the other inhumanities that are so common among us today. Well, we simply must look elsewhere for our conviction about the meaning of life.

If we were to pass out three-by-five cards to a group of people and ask each one to write on it his or her own idea of the meaning of life, I suspect that the dictionary definition, "life is the period from birth to death," would be the most common response. From what I am reading and observing, it appears that most people are merely drifting along through life (the period from birth to death) with no purpose at all—except to extend that period from birth to death.

Even Benjamin Franklin is quoted as saying that "time is the stuff that life is made of." And while that is true, it is only partly true. There's more to life than the time factor. We're hearing a lot these days about "the quality of life," which would indicate after more thought there must be something more to it than mere existence. Robert Whitaker has written a little poem that says:

Live for something; have a purpose,
And that purpose keep in view;
Drifting like a helpless vessel,
Thou canst ne'er to life be true.

Half the wrecks that strew life's ocean,
If some star had been their guide,
Might have now been riding safely,
But, they drifted with the tide.

Live for something, and live in earnest,
By the world of men unnoticed,
Though the work may humble be,
Known alone to God and thee.

Every Act has priceless value;
To the Architect of fate:
'Tis the spirit of thy doing
That alone will make it great.

Live for something—God and angels
Are thy watchers in the strife,
And above the smoke and conflict
Gleams the victor's crown of life.

Live for something; God has given
Freely of His stores divine;
Richest gifts of earth and heaven,
If thou willest, may be thine.

Fundamental to a healthy view of life is a person's perception of his own identity: "Who am I?" then the question,
"What am I doing here?" David, in the Eighth Psalm asked:

When I consider thy heavens, the work of thy fingers,
the moon and the stars, which thou hast ordained; what
is man, that thou art mindful of him? and the son of man
that thou visitest him?

David's shepherd-life gave him ample opportunity to scan
the lofty heavens at night and consider the radiant moon and
the hosts of sparkling stars as the work of God's fingers. Filled
with wonder and marvelous condescension, he thinks, "What
is man" that he should be so favored of God?

Then, it seems that with but a moment's reflection, he remembers the words of Genesis 1:26, 27:

> And God said, Let us make man in our own image, after
> our likeness. . . . So God created man in his own image,
> in the image of God created he him; male and female
> created he them.

Then David adds, "Thou hast made him a little lower than the angels [actually only a little lower than God], and hast crowned him with glory and honor." The greatest indignity and insult we can make against God is to take the life of another person, because he bears the very image of God himself. It is because of that crown of glory and honor that, in Genesis 9:6, God pronounced the death penalty on the murderer. God crowned man with glory and majesty when He gave him the nature that is just short of deity itself.

The unbeliever deceives and demeans us when he says we are "social animals," a direct product of the earth, that we owe our origin entirely to certain physical and chemical properties of the ancient earth, and that nothing supernatural was involved—only time and natural, physical, and chemical laws operating within the peculiarly suitable earthly environment. No, my friend, we are not "social animals," we are the off-spring of God—that's who we are. You and I are the offspring of God, and we must never, never, never lose sight of it, because it's as Eleanor Roosevelt said, "Life has to be lived," and our self-perception will determine how we live it.

My friend, the real meaning of life is found in a purpose which is bigger than life itself. But what on earth could that be? Could it be pleasure, entertainment, fun? Could it be possessions or power or success?

A few years ago Dr. Frank Pack of Pepperdine University co-authored a book with Dr. Prentice Meador on the subject of preaching. In it he told of a faculty member of a large eastern university who for some fourteen years had begun his lectures to about a hundred and forty students by asking them to bow their heads and think seriously about whether there was anything or anybody for which each of them might give his or her life. If the answer was yes, they were to raise their hands. He reported that the percentage had not varied over those fourteen years—one out of ten. Only ten percent knew of anything for which they would give their lives. I'm reminded of what Jesus said in Matthew 16:25: "For whosoever will save his life shall lose it: and whosoever will lose his life for my sake shall find it."

Now, we're getting somewhere. Life has meaning when we have found the purpose that is bigger than life itself. I think of the apostle Paul, whose life was so totally spent for Jesus' sake, who prayed that "Christ shall be magnified in my body, whether it be by life, or by death" (Philippians 1:20). And he added, "For me to live is Christ, and to die is gain." That's the way it should be with every Christian. But the unbeliever, even the uncommitted church member, may have a problem with understanding him. My friend, he's simply saying that for him, and for all Christians, life is not simply a matter of "the period from birth to death"; it isn't just "being alive," or even striving to get ahead, or being a success, or making a name for oneself. It isn't owning lands and houses and cattle and oil wells and automobiles or amassing a large estate to pass on to the next generation; that isn't what life is all about. Life isn't just "being good and doing good" as important as that is. Rather it is to do what we do, and be what we are for Christ. It is to so totally lose our time, our energies, our talents, and our prosperity in Him that Christ may be glorified in our bodies whether by life or by death.

John said of Jesus,

> In the beginning was the Word, and the Word was with God, and the Word was God. The same was in the beginning with God. All things were made by him; and without him was not any thing made that was made. In him was life; and the life was the light of men (John 1:4).

When in John 10:10 Jesus said that, as the Good Shepherd, He "came that they might have life, and have it more abundantly," He was not saying that He came to give us an abundance of material wealth and physical health as it's often preached today, but to give fullness to our life—to add a dimension to our existence. This is seen in John 17:1-3, too. The Bible says,

> These words spake Jesus, and lifted up his eyes to heaven, and said, Father, the hour is come; glorify thy Son, that thy Son also may glorify thee: as thou hast given him power over all flesh, that he should give eternal life to as many as thou hast given him. And this is life eternal [eternal life], that they might know thee the only true God, and Jesus Christ, whom thou hast sent.

We're so accustomed to thinking of "eternal life" as life that goes on for ever, that it's easy to miss the point here. "Eternal" when used with "life" speaks not just to quantity but also to quality. Barclay concludes from it: "Life is only of value when it is nothing less than the life of God—and that," he says, "is the meaning of eternal life." To illustrate the idea, he draws on a story told by the ancient Greeks of

> . . . Aurora, the goddess of dawn, who fell in love with Tithonus, the mortal youth. Zeus offered her any gift she might choose for her mortal lover. She asked that Tithonus might never die; but she forgot to ask that he might remain for ever young. So Tithonus lived for ever growing older and older and more and more decrepit, till life became a terrible and intolerable curse.

That quality of life included in the word *eternal* is that "abundance" which Jesus said He came to bring us. It's part of that newness of life of which the Bible speaks when in Romans 6:3, 4 it says,

> Know ye not, that so many of us as were baptized into Jesus Christ were baptized into his death? Therefore we are buried with him by baptism into death: that like as Christ was raised up from the dead by the glory of the Father, even so we also should walk in newness of life.

And in II Corinthians 5:17 when it says, "Therefore if any man be in Christ, he is a new creature: old things are passed away; behold, all things are become new." It isn't new *just* from the point of a new beginning, but it is a new kind of life, a life with God, life in abundance with meaning and direction.

In the long ago God spoke some very meaningful words through Jeremiah the prophet. He said,

> Let not the wise man glory in his wisdom, neither let the mighty man glory in his might, let not the rich man glory in his riches: but let him that glorieth glory in this, that he understandeth and knoweth me . . . saith the Lord.

Christ came that we may know God, and that, my friend, is the meaning of life. It is in God that (1) we live (He is the fountain of life), (2) we move (we are motivated by him to be all we are and do all we do) and (3) we have our being (or our identity as His offspring).

I came upon this poem that says it well. I don't know who wrote it. My source didn't give credit. It says,

> Lord, it belongs not to my care
> Whether I die or live;
> To love and serve Thee is my share
> And this Thy grace must give.
>
> If life be long, I will be glad,
> That I may long obey;
> If short—then why should I be sad
> To soar to endless day?

God bless you. I love you.

QUESTIONS FOR CLASS DISCUSSION

1. What is life?

2. What is fundamental to a healthy view of life?

3. How does meaning add importance to life?

4. List some things for which you would die. Some people.

5. Discuss the idea of "life eternal" as Jesus spoke of it in John 17:3.

2

Life is
Worth Living

Philippians 1:15-21

Some indeed preach Christ even of envy and strife; and some also of good will: the one preach Christ of contention, not sincerely, supposing to add affliction to my bonds: but the other of love, knowing that I am set for the defence of the gospel. What then? notwithstanding, every way, whether in pretence, or in truth, Christ is preached; and I therein do rejoice, yea, and will rejoice. For I know that this shall turn to my salvation through your prayer, and the supply of the Spirit of Jesus Christ, according to my earnest expectation and my hope, that in nothing I shall be ashamed, but that with all boldness, as always, so now also Christ shall be magnified in my body, whether it be by life, or by death. For to me to live is Christ, and to die is gain.

A small boy said to his dad, "After all, I didn't ask to be born." "I know," said his dad, "and if you had, the answer would have been no!" We get a chuckle out of that, but it's true. Some unknown sage has said, "You came not into the world because you chose, or when you chose, but because the world had need of you." I often paraphrase that: "You came not into the world because you chose or when you chose, but because God had need of you."

What is life all about? What are we doing here? Is there any real purpose in the universe? Is there any meaning in life? Scientific materialism says no. Humanism says only as we create and develop our futures here. Is it any wonder, then, that many people are asking, "Is life worth living?"

In an era when there are more people living on this planet than at any time in its history, and in a generation when more people are living longer, the question of the purpose and the meaning of life is more relevant than about any other question I can think of that has to do with human existence.

Suicide is the tenth leading cause of death in America. We are killing ourselves at the rate of seventy-five a day, or one about every twenty minutes. Many, many more attempt to do so, but fail. Of course no one will ever know for sure, but people who have made a study of these things tell us that someone tries to commit suicide every minute of the day around the clock. That means that there are something like one-half million people every year who, for various and sundry reasons, have lost the sense of purpose and meaning in their lives and decided it isn't worth it. Thank God many of them fail in the attempt to end life, because many of them get back on course and continue very productive and meaningful lives.

Almost as sad as that is the fact that millions more who would never entertain the thought of suicide have lived all their lives without the slightest idea of the meaning of it or what they are doing here. What a waste!

John Wanamaker told a story about how his father went about hiring a new foreman for his lumber yard. Three men had applied for the job. They were assigned the task of moving a pile of bricks from one corner of the lumber yard to another. When they were finished, Mr. Wanamaker told them to move the bricks back to where they were. That went on all day—from one corner of the yard to the other and back again. Back and forth all day long.

At the end of the day, the men were paid off and told to come back tomorrow. But one of them said, "I need work, but I won't be back. I will not work without a purpose!" Needless to say, he got the job of leading other men. But the point is that many of us are living life like men moving a pile of bricks from one corner of the lumber yard to another and back again, while others must—and they do—see a purpose in life.

What is *your* life? What are *you* doing here? Now, people are going to answer that in many different ways. Do you remember Bobby Fisher? Well, a few years ago Bobby Fisher was the world's greatest chess player. He defeated Boris Spassky of the Soviet Union to become the world champion chess player. It's said that in an interview one time, he made the statement, "Chess is life." It would have to be to become world champion, wouldn't it? Well, what is *your* life? Is it *chess?* It isn't likely.

To be perfectly honest, some people will have to answer, "It's pleasure." (Some not so honest won't say it, but it is true nonetheless.) Say it or not, that is the sole reason for their existence. "You only go 'round once, so go with all the gusto you can get." That's the philosophy of literally millions of people in our society. You see it expressed in many ways and places. I saw it on a church bulletin board recently: a poster with the message, "Kids just wanna have fun." Kids aren't the only ones. The Epicureans whom the apostle Paul confronted in the city of Athens (Acts 17:22-34) were saying, "Eat, drink and be merry, for tomorrow you die" (I Corinthians 15:32). Even King Solomon, many centuries before Christ, subscribed to that idea for awhile. He said,

> There is nothing better for a man, than that he should eat and drink, and that he should make his soul enjoy good in his labor. This also I saw, that it was from the hand of God (Ecclesiastes 2:24).

I have a book; it's a rather small book (seventy-five pages or so) titled, *Is Life Worth Living?* It's a debate between two brilliant men of a few years past: Dr. Frederick Starr, a professor of anthropology at the University of Illinois and Clarence Darrow, the eloquent lawyer, platform speaker, and debater who is best known for his part in the famous *Scopes Monkey Trial* in Tennessee in 1925. Both of these men were agnostics. (They didn't know whether God exists or not.) Dr. Starr argued that life is worth living and Mr. Darrow denied it. It's an interesting exchange of views for many reasons. One of them is that Dr. Starr argued that life is worth living because of its pleasures. And that Clarence Darrow had no difficulty at all showing that if that is man's purpose on this planet, at any time his sorrows exceed his pleasures, life is no longer worth living. And he's right, isn't he? There *must* be more to life than a merry-go-round, don't you think?

Dr. Starr came right back with the argument that life is worth living because of *the money* a person can make and have and keep and count—the wealth he can accrue. Oh, there are millions of people who would agree with that. It isn't that they have any hopes of being millionaires necessarily, but that possessions possess them.

Just recently I was reading about a lady who died on March 30, 1975. The article gave her name, but I'd better not do that here. Everybody acquainted with the situation thought she was just another poverty victim. She had wasted away to a mere fifty-pound skeleton by the time social workers took her to the hospital. Two days before she died, an appointed attorney found two safe deposit box keys in the hovel that she had inhabited for more than twenty-five years, and in those boxes they found $799,581.50. For years she had been living off the food and clothing that neighbors and others had been bringing in, while all her money went into those safe deposit boxes. And she died, not of poverty but of greed. Is that living? Imagine starving to death with more than three quarters of a million dollars in the bank. "Well," someone says, "it isn't the money that gives meaning to life, it's the things money can buy and do for us."

Have you seen the bumper sticker that says: "He who dies with the most toys wins"? Is that what life is all about? Is life to be measured by one's ability to accumulate toys? That word *toys* puts a different light on things, doesn't it? I guess we just hadn't thought of them as toys. I wonder how many of our "necessities" are really and truly just "toys." Jesus had something to say about that. "Take heed," He said, "and beware of covetousness: for a man's life consisteth not in the abundance of the toys (pardon me, I mean *things*) which he possesseth" (Luke 12:15). Yes, that's what He said, "A man's life consists not of the abundance of the things which he possesses."

In response to the question, "What is your life?" some people might answer, "To have gained recognition and been acclaimed a success, that's what life is all about—*succeeding.*" Like the other things which we've mentioned, this idea isn't all bad, but to make it the sole meaning and purpose for living, is a mistake, for such a life is fraught with disappointment. In the Olympic Games of ancient Greece, the laurel wreath was awarded the winner instead of the gold, silver, or bronze medals in our times. Therefore, the laurel wreath or crown was a much coveted prize; it was the sign of a champion, but it was very temporal. It wilted and faded very quickly, then it was gone.

No, the Bible doesn't encourage slothfulness and failure. It's a book for winners. As a matter of fact, it's been called the ultimate how-to book for success. I don't know whether you have read the last chapter, but if so, you know that the Christians win! So I suppose the real question is, "In what do you want to be recognized, acclaimed, and remembered as a winner?"

It's reported that as baseball's great, Ty Cobb, was leaving a banquet hall where he had been recognized and honored a man said to him, "It must be a source of great joy and pride to you to receive such praise as you have heard tonight, and to know that you have given entertainment as a ballplayer to so many thousands of people." Cobb replied, "I wish I had been a doctor. To have been able to heal diseases and relieve people of pain would have meant far more to me than the cheers and plaudits of the thousands in the baseball parks."

So I guess it is a matter of what is going to be the source of greatest satisfaction when our striving here is ended. I read of the fellow who was so proud of his bowling score that he wanted it inscribed on his tombstone, "He bowled 300." Well,

I am sorry folks; I'll never be able to share his enthusiasm. With my kind of bowling, I'll never know the joy of bowling 300, but I can't imagine that being the most meaningful accomplishment of my life when I come to lay my trophies at the feet of the Master of men. I think I'll want something more than that, don't you?

The apostle Paul, who is a tremendously powerful example of Christian thought on this subject, declared in that passage which we're using as our scripture text today, "To me to live is Christ." Awhile ago, we mentioned that chess champion Bobby Fisher said, "Chess is life." And when he was asked what chess meant to him, he thought it over for a full sixty seconds, then he replied, "Everything!" So it is with Paul. To him, to live is Christ. Christ is everything! Others may live for fun or fortune or fame, but the Christian is different—at least he should be. He lives for a far more noble and lasting purpose. The Christian says, "In nothing shall I be ashamed, but that with all boldness, as always, so now also Christ shall be magnified in my body, whether it be by life, or by death" (Philippians 1:20).

Paul was a violent persecutor of the church of Christ. We are introduced to him in Acts 7 where he is consenting to the death of Stephen, the first Christian martyr. There is no doubt that he had a great part in the persecution that came upon the Jerusalem church that we read about in Acts 8 which resulted in the disciples' scattering to distant cities. In the opening verses of chapter 9, we are told that Saul was pursuing these disciples even to as far away as Damascus, Syria and bringing them back to Jerusalem, bound to imprison them. As he approached the city, a great light shined upon him, and a voice said to him,

> Saul, Saul, why persecutest thou me? And he said, Who art thou, Lord? And the Lord said, I am Jesus whom thou persecutest: it is hard for thee to kick against the pricks. And he trembling and astonished said, *Lord, what wilt thou have me to do* (Acts 9:4-6)?

We have generally thought that Saul was enquiring about

what to do to be saved, and I'm sure that's right as far as it goes, but it goes further than that. I am convinced he was also asking what the Lord wanted him to do with the rest of his life. He was conscientiously and zealously trying to rid the world of the church at the time (Acts 23:1; Galatians 1:14), thinking surely this was the will of God for his life. Obviously, it was not. Then, "Lord, what wilt thou have me to do?"

When a person becomes a Christian like Saul did, he not only experiences a change of heart by faith, a change of behavior by repentance, a change of commitment by his confession of Christ, and a change of his relationship with God by baptism, he must also experience a change of purpose for living. Pleasure, possessions, or prominence no longer dominate and control his life, but Jesus Christ and His ministry to the world. Such a conversion (or change) is not merely saying, "Lord Jesus, come into my heart," but it is a commitment of all a person *is* and *has* to Christ and His work.

Life consists of five elements: (1) time, (2) talent, (3) energy, (4) productivity, and (5) purpose. And the Christian's commitment to Christ is his whole life—his time, his talent, his energy, and his productivity—all of it. Jesus said,

> Whosoever will save his life [his time here, his talent, his energy, his productivity], shall lose it: and whosoever shall lose his life [his three-score years and ten, his gift or skill, his healthy body, and his earnings] for my sake shall find it. For what is a man profited, if he shall gain the whole world, and lose his own soul? or what shall a man give in exchange for his soul (Matthew 16:24-26)?

According to an article in the November 1986 issue of *Psychology Today*, a study conducted by University of Akron sociologist Margaret Poloma revealed that people who feel close to God on a personal basis have a deeper sense of purpose and are happier with their health. Poloma says, "Religion has been under emphasized as a factor leading to life satisfaction." The study which she presented to the American Sociological Association also suggested that religious identity is the most important factor in a person's finding happiness in life—even more important than job success or family. We would hope you would consider it today.

God bless you. I love you.

QUESTIONS FOR CLASS DISCUSSION

1. Discuss the relevancy of the question, "Is Life Worth Living?"

2. Talk about some of the trivial things in which people have tried to find reason for living and show the futility in them.

3. What is the greatest known factor leading to the satisfaction with life?

4. What would you like to have inscribed on your grave stone?

5. What makes life worth living?

3

Christians are Sojourners

I Peter 2:11

Dearly beloved, I beseech you as strangers and pilgrims, abstain from fleshly lusts, which war against the soul.

It doesn't matter who we are or what our fortune may be in this world, all of us find life a bit difficult at times. There just are disappointments, defeats, discouragements, death, and a whole horde of other things that interrupt the smooth ongoing of life. Some folks tell us that if you will become a Christian, God will take away all those things and you can live healthy and wealthy and free from all of life's annoyances. But it isn't true and God doesn't promise it. However, the word of God is just chock full of some very rich encouragements—some exceedingly great and precious promises—for the Christian, so that in spite of all the negatives, the child of God can live life to the very fullest.

Not the least of these encouragements is the assurance that the Christian is but a sojourner in this world, en route to a better place. This world is not his home; he's only passing through and the sufferings of this present world are not to be compared with the joy that shall be his when he reaches his final destiny.

The message of I Peter is "hope." It is written to the Christians who are addressed in the very first verse as scattered strangers or "sojourners of the dispersion," most likely Jews by birth, but not necessarily so, who were routed from their homeland by persecution and were scattered throughout the various provinces of what we call Asia Minor. They knew suffering first hand. And Peter has a lot to say about that, but his theme is "hope."

Following that brief salutation and thanksgiving there is, as is customary in so many of the epistles, a section of doctrinal teaching about salvation by the grace of God in Christ Jesus. Doctrine (theology, if you prefer) is important, my friend. Some people are turned off by it, but it is essential and always precedes practical exhortations in Scripture. A person is and does what he has been taught. Peter reminded them (and us) that by the abundant mercy of God, Christians have been begotten again unto a living hope by the resurrection of Jesus Christ to an incorruptible, undefiled inheritance, the beauty of which never fades, which is reserved in heaven for them. That hope will bloom into full reality in the last day—when Jesus comes. That's what critics and materialists, unbelievers who want their pie now, call "pie-in-the-sky religion." If that's what it is, so be it.

Then there follows a series of exhortations to holy living, brotherly love, and growth as the people of God until we come to the two verses that constitute our text in which the inspired writer returns to the metaphors of "strangers" (sojourners) and "pilgrims." In these figures all who read the passage, whether in that first century or our own, will find courage and hope in the ups-and-downs of this life.

With this analogy Peter is saying that Christians are not of this world; they are different. They are citizens of another country and subjects of another King. They are like Abraham who,

> when he was called to go out into a place which he should
> after receive for an inheritance, obeyed; and he went out,

not knowing whither he went. By faith he sojourned in the land of promise, as in a strange country, dwelling in tabernacles with Isaac and Jacob, the heirs with him of the same promise: for he looked for a city which hath foundations, whose builder and maker is God (Hebrews 11:8-10).

In His prayer recorded in John 17, Jesus said His disciples were in the world but they were not of the world. Paul also uses the analogy in his letter to the Philippian Christians when he says, "Our conversation [or our citizenship] is in heaven from whence we also look for the Savior, the Lord Jesus Christ" (Philippians 3:20).

From all of this we can learn a number of things that should be helpful to us in our sojourn in the world as a strange land. Among other things, we learn not to drive down our stakes, or homestead here, because we're only passing through to a better land. We must not become so attached to this world that we're not ready to leave it behind and go on. We'll not take any of it with us when we leave—not one acre of it—so if we should make it our aim and purpose in life to acquire as much of the world as we can in our allotted time, we will ultimately be the loser. To show the utter futility of it, Jesus asked, "What is a man profited, if he shall gain the whole world, and lose his own soul? or what shall a man give in exchange for his soul" (Matthew 16:26)?

We are told in I John 2:15, "Love not the world." The focus of the Christian life is not on the material success and prosperity that is so often the heart of modern popular preaching. Paul expressed it well in II Corinthians 4:18, "We look not at the things which are seen, but at the things which are not seen:" he said, "for the things which are seen are temporal; but the things which are not seen are eternal."

Back in the 1960s my family and I were sojourners in Australia. The people there received us warmly and we enjoyed living among them. Despite the fact that our speech and many of our customs were different from theirs, we could have easily adjusted and lived there very comfortably the rest of our lives. We were offered the opportunity, and I'm sure we could have obtained Australian citizenship. But we loved America. It was our real home and we planned someday to return, so we maintained our American citizenship. And we didn't buy up a lot of real estate and make a lot of alliances and binding commitments that would hinder us when the time came for us to come home. So it should be with the Christian in this world.

Closely akin to that thought is the idea of travelling lightly. I mean, don't take too much baggage. One of the best things that has happened to air travellers in recent months is the regulation restricting each passenger to two carry-on bags. Why, I have seen people board an airplane with so many clothes bags, boxes, parcels, satchels, and stuff they could hardly make it down the aisle to their seats, haven't you?

Several years ago I co-hosted a tour of the Bible lands. And in preparation we wrote several letters of *do*'s and *don't*'s to each person we had recruited for the trip. One of the things we stressed heavily was to take only two bags—check one and carry one—travel light. And after all of that, one day while we were flying over Egypt, one lady told me she had brought along twelve pairs of shoes. That was almost one pair for every day of the trip. I asked her how many pairs she had worn and she said, "One." But she had to lug all those others around everywhere we went—excess baggage. Some people seem to think the purpose of life is to accumulate at least one and perhaps many of every "thing" that comes along, most of which is only excess baggage and a hindrance on the journey to Heaven. In that passage I mentioned a moment ago (I John 2:15) in which John said, "Love not the world," he added, "neither the *things* of the world," because they are only going to get in the way.

This principle also applies to the *ways* of the world. Peter says in our text, "Abstain from fleshly lusts, which war against the soul." Some things are legal here, acceptable to the world, even respectable, which would only be counter-productive to the Christian whose purpose it is to go home to Heaven at the end of the journey. Drinking, extra-marital sex, homosexuality, gambling, abortion—all of these, and you can think of others, though legal and acceptable—are fleshly lusts that war against the soul. There are other things that may be harmless in themselves, but they will become a burden and have the same effect.

Christians are to be separate from the world (II Corinthians 6:10). They are to have no part in the unfruitful works of darkness, but rather reprove them (Ephesians 5:11). They are to live lives becoming the name they wear. And it isn't enough just to be a non-participant in evil around them, Christians must "reprove" them or speak out against them as well. Because I know I'm just passing this way to my eternal home, and such ways of the world would only be a hindrance, I can resist temptation to all such worldly lifestyles.

As a pilgrim whose citizenship is in Heaven, I can also know that the natives of this strange land through which I pass may be hostile toward me at times. They may say some very ugly and mean things about me, some of which may even be untrue; they may even persecute me. Our text says,

> Having our conversation [lifestyle] honest among the Gentiles: that whereas they speak against you as evildoers, they may by your good works, which they shall behold [see], glorify God in the day of visitation.

Very often we have mail from viewers who ask what recourse they have. Someone is circulating lies about them and they have been unable to do anything about it. My friend, Peter offers you the only recourse I know. You just live as honestly and uprightly as you know how, so that no one will believe the liar, and when the truth does come out—and it will, it may take years but believe me, it will come out—you will be vindicated and God will be glorified in your behavior. Take heart in the words of the Master, my friend. He said,

> The disciple is not above his master, nor the servant above his lord. It is enough for the disciple that he be as

his master, and the servant as his lord. If they have
called the master of the house Beelzebub, how much
more shall they call them of his household (Matthew
10:24, 25)?

And since a Christian is a sojourner, he receives strength
from the hope he has of something better. He can endure
hardships; he can handle the disappointments, the discouragements, and defeats that come his way, knowing they are only
temporary and there is coming a better life. Paul put it this
way:

> We are troubled on every side, yet not distressed; we are
> perplexed, but not in despair; persecuted, but not for-
> saken; cast down, but not destroyed; always bearing
> about in the body the dying of the Lord Jesus, that the
> life also of Jesus might be made manifest in our body. . . .
> For which cause we faint not; but though our outward
> man perish, yet the inward man is renewed day by day.
> For our light affliction, which is but for a moment,
> worketh for us a far more exceeding and eternal weight
> of glory (II Corinthians 4:8-10, 11-13).

Finally, the pilgrim must never lose his love for home. He
must never take his eyes off Heaven. He wants above all else to
go home. There's a beautiful passage in Colossians; it's in
chapter 3, beginning with verse 1 and it says,

> If ye then be risen with Christ, seek those things which
> are above, where Christ sitteth on the right hand of God.
> Set your affection on things above, not on things on the
> earth. For ye are dead, and your life is hid with Christ in
> God.

Of course, Colossians is written to Christians. In verse 12 of
the preceding chapter, Paul had written that they had been
"buried with him in baptism, wherein also ye are risen with
him," he said, "through the faith of the operation of God, who
hath raised him from the dead."

Now he's saying if (or since) you are raised up with Christ,
keep seeking the things above, where Christ is seated at the

right hand of God. My friend, Heaven is real. This passage says Christ is now seated at the right hand of God and in Philippians 3:20, he declares that our citizenship is in Heaven whence we also eagerly wait for the Savior, the Lord Jesus Christ. Christ is seated at the right hand of God in Heaven. So keep on seeking those things above, not the things of the earth. And "set your affections [your love] on the things above." Don't lose your love for Heaven. Above all things, more important than anything else, get ready and be ready to go to Heaven when the time comes.

If you have not already done so, hasten to do as the Colossian Christians had done. Be buried with Him and raised with Him in baptism and so begin your heavenward journey at once.

Every day the mail brings me letters from people who are despairing of life. Some of them have turned to drugs and alcohol for relief from those frustrations and anxieties; others to psychoanalysis or psychiatry; and others have even considered suicide as a way out. On the other hand, there is never a day passes that we don't hear from people who have found comfort and the courage they need to face the realities of living through faith in our living and loving God. Such passages of Scripture as we have studied here provide the salvation, reinforcement, and reassurance they need to face life triumphantly. I strongly recommend that faith to you, my friend.

God bless you. I love you.

QUESTIONS FOR CLASS DISCUSSION

1. What is a "sojourner"? In what ways are Christians sojourners in life?

2. What suggestions would you have for sojourners in a strange land?

3. Explain why Christians cannot become involved in some of the socially accepted or politically correct lifestyles of the world in which he sojourns.

4. What can a Christian do to defend himself, his integrity, and his good name when the world vilifies him?

5. Explain how the Christian faith enables a person to live life victoriously in an evil world where he sojourns.

4

The Problem
of Suffering

We have suffered some severe natural tragedies in recent
months: the hurricane that hit the east coast, the terrible
flooding in the central states, and the devastating earthquake
in India that claimed so many, many lives, and many more
were injured. Untold numbers of people suffered material loss
in the destruction of their homes and businesses. And the
emotional suffering is immeasurable. There is no way for someone such as I, so distantly removed from the actual scenes, to
understand, not to mention describe the pain, the destruction,
the loss, the devastation hundreds of thousands of people suffered in those disasters. We thank God for the great out-
pouring of benevolent hearts to the victims.

In addition to those nationally publicized emergencies, there
is the daily travail of millions of families in such a wide variety
of ways it's impossible to imagine or describe them. Having
preached and ministered to people on a person-to-person basis

for many years, I thought when I began this television ministry I was familiar with most of the ways people suffer. But my! Oh my! what an eye-opener this has been. You should hear some of our telephone calls and read some of our mail. I have remarked to my wife and others on many occasions that it seems some people have more than their fair share of misfortune and misery.

And these are not wicked people; they're upright, God-fearing people and good families, many of them. They don't understand why those things happen to them, and quite frankly, neither do I. We are addressing the problem of suffering, not as a philosophical argument for the existence of God, but on how to cope with it when it comes our way.

One of the questions we are most often asked is why good people must suffer the pain of affliction or sickness or bereavement or disappointment or rejection or frustration of some kind. That has been a troublesome question for believers and unbelievers alike for millenniums. If God is an all-powerful and all-loving personal Being as He is said to be in the Scriptures, why does He permit it to be so? Doesn't He care that innocent babies are born into this world with crippling defects, paralyzed, deformed, and maimed? Can't He stop the abuse and destruction of helpless little children either before birth or after? Why doesn't He intervene in the lives of good people so as to protect them or deliver them from tragic accidents and prolonged illnesses that so completely drain families of their physical, financial, emotional, and even their spiritual resources? Or, is He powerless to do anything about such things?

Well, there are no easy answers. The fellow who thinks he knows all the answers is sure to be proven wrong. Job's friends thought they knew. Personally, I have always found comfort in the fact that some of the people in the Bible who lived and worked closest with God were some who seemed to have suffered greatly and even unjustly. There were Joseph and Moses and Job and Elijah and John the Baptist and Peter and James and Paul and the apostle John, exiled on Patmos for the word of God, not to mention the Son of God Himself. You could name others, I am sure, which all goes to show that, in spite of the "gospel of health and wealth" that is being preached all over the country, becoming a child of God and living for Him doesn't immunize a person from suffering.

Often it's easy to explain anything that happens to us as being, "God's will," but we need to be careful about that. Not everything is arbitrarily the will of God for our lives. Some things may be the working of Satan. Job's terrible afflictions, for example, were the working Satan (Job 2:4-7). And in Luke 13:11-17 there is the woman whom Jesus healed who had been "bowed together" or "bent over" so that she couldn't straighten up, whom Satan had bound for eighteen years.

But listen to me carefully now, my friend. If some terrible tragedy should strike you or your family, you beware of and avoid that person who tells you that it is because you are possessed of the devil. I can conceive of no better way of compounding the problem of human suffering than by telling the afflicted person it is because he is demon possessed! I don't mind telling you, it angers me to hear that some self-styled spirit-filled prophet has told a poor distraught, agonizing soul that he has a devil. It could possibly be true, but it probably is not true!

Then, some of our suffering may be of our own doing. God has made us with free will, the exercise of which may bring evil as well as good on ourselves or on those whose lives are affected by ours. We are free to act carelessly or thoughtlessly. Most accidents are the result of carelessness or thoughtlessness. If the person or persons involved had been more alert or cautious, much suffering could have been avoided. We are also free to act ignorantly, and we often suffer for it. We just don't know any better than to do some of the things we do from which we suffer terrible consequences. We are free to act deceitfully and maliciously.

Cain maliciously murdered his brother Abel (Genesis 4:1-15). Jacob deceitfully obtained the blessing that belonged to his brother Esau (Genesis 27). David acted deceitfully to cause Uriah's death and was as guilty as if he had committed the deed himself (II Samuel 11:14-21). Much of the evil in the world is because people choose to be vicious and mean to one another. And we are free to sin, which is the cause of—not all but very much of—our suffering. The Bible says, "The way of transgressors is hard" (Proverbs 13:15). Again it says, "Many sorrows shall be to the wicked" (Psalm 32:10), and it has been demonstrated over and over again in our own experiences. "Be not deceived; God is not mocked: for whatsoever a man soweth, that shall he also reap" (Galatians 6:7).

God gave man this freedom of will, knowing well that it involved the possibility of man's making wrong choices and suffering for it. But He was willing to take that risk so He might deal with us through persuasion, not force, not as robots, but as moral and spiritual persons like Himself. By His creating us so, He imposed a limitation upon Himself to always have His way and do His will in our lives.

Leslie D. Weatherhead wrote a little book back some years ago which he titled *The Will of God* in which he discussed this matter of God's will. He explained the difference between God's *intentional* will and His *circumstantial* will. God's intentional will for us, he said, is God's ideal plan or purpose for our lives. His circumstantial will is His will for us within the limited circumstances or conditions resulting from our wrong choices that make His intentional will impractical or impossible—sort of making the best of a situation which we may have created ourselves. So sometimes what appears to be a tragedy may very well be His circumstantial will for us.

Since we know that suffering is a part of life—the Scripture says, "Man that is born of woman is of few days, and full of trouble" (Job 14:1), and both Scripture and experience teach us that even the righteous are not free or exempt from it—let's look at some of its blessings and see if we can profit from it.

First, God takes things that are of themselves bad and works good from them. Sometimes we hear modern miracle workers saying, "It is God's will for you to be healthy and happy." My friend, it isn't necessarily so. Augustine, fifth century theologian-philosopher said, "God judged it better to bring good out of evil than to suffer no evil to exist."

In some instances the sufferer experiences more of God's grace than had he never suffered. Matthew Henry, respected scholar and author, a man of the Methodist faith said, "Extraordinary afflictions are not always the punishment of extraordinary sins, but sometimes the trial of extraordinary grace." This is exactly what Paul is saying about his own condition in II Corinthians 12:8, 9. "For this thing I besought the Lord thrice, [three times] that it might depart from me," he said. Wasn't it God's will for Paul to be free of his affliction? Wasn't Paul a man of faith? If God willed it and Paul believed it, why didn't God heal him? Listen to God's answer in the next verse: "My grace is sufficient for thee: for my strength is made perfect in weakness." The sufferer experiences more of God's grace and power by living with the problem. I have had suffering people say, "You never know how much you can endure until you're forced to do it." But where do they get the grace to endure? Well, God has said, "My grace is sufficient for thee."

Next, there is a purpose in suffering. The number of Christians who have spent more time in prison than the apostle Paul would be very small, wouldn't you say? Why do you suppose the Lord would permit this very godly and zealous man to languish in a prison cell? Why didn't He deliver him—set him free—and put him out to travelling as Paul was willing to do, to preach the gospel where no other person had gone? There must have been a purpose in it!

When I see ardent, talented, people with a real grasp on the purpose and meaning of life confined to a wheel chair or shut in, I wonder why this has to happen to them? Why not some of the others of us who are more limited and less committed instead of them? And my only answer is that, had Paul been free to travel and preach, he might never have had the time to write all the epistles he did. Perhaps God kept him shut up in

prison for a purpose. Those letters Paul wrote in his prison
cells have had far more lasting effect on the church and civilization than the sermons he might have preached would have.

Then too, the sufferer enjoys more of the presence of God. I
keep coming back to Paul as an example, but he suffered so
much in so many ways, he seems to be typical of much of what
we are talking about. In the last letter he wrote—it was from
his prison cell in Rome to Timothy—and he said,

> At my first answer no man stood with me, but all men
> forsook me: I pray God that it may not be laid to their
> charge. Notwithstanding the Lord stood with me, and
> strengthened me; that by me the preaching might be
> fully known, and that all the Gentiles might hear: and I
> was delivered out of the mouth of the lion. And the Lord
> shall deliver me from every evil work, and will preserve
> me unto his heavenly kingdom: to whom be glory for
> ever and ever. Amen.

Many people can relate to that. Some of the greatest pain a
person can know is when friends forsake and there is no one to
stand by. And out of the depth of that pain, the Christian
learns that the Lord stands with him and gives strength. He is
"the Father of mercies, and the God of all comfort, who
comforteth us in all our tribulation [or affliction]." Yes, there
are things worse than death. One of them is the betrayal of a
trusted friend. But even then the Lord stands by. He never
leaves or forsakes us (Hebrews 13:5).

Suffering also refines character. Lives immersed in tragedy
are not merely touched, but they are turned 180 degrees in
their course. The dross of pride and self-glory and vanity and
presumptuousness are purged in the smeltering furnace of
affliction. Adversity is the garden in which bloom humility and
patience and fortitude and thanksgiving and trust and hope. So
Paul says in Romans 5:3, 4, "We glory in tribulations also:
knowing that tribulation worketh patience; and patience, experience; and experience, hope."

No discussion of the subject of suffering would be complete

without reference to at least one other passage that bears strongly on it. It's II Corinthians 4:17 and it says, "For our light affliction, which is but for a moment, worketh for us a far more exceeding and eternal weight of glory." Whatever may be the extent of our suffering, it is light and but for a moment when it is compared with the eternal weight of glory which awaits the Christian sufferer in heaven. The whole story of suffering can't be seen from this side. Accordingly someone has written a poem and titled it *The Weaver* in which he (she) has said,

> My life is but a weaving
>   Between my Lord and me.
> I cannot choose the colors
>   He worketh steadily.
>
> Ofttimes He weaveth sorrow,
>   And I, in foolish pride,
> Forget He sees the upper
>   And I, the underside.
>
> Not till the loom is silent
>   And the shuttles cease to fly
> Shall God unroll the canvas
>   And explain the reason why.
>
> The dark threads are as needful
>   In the Weaver's skillful hand
> As the threads of gold and silver
>   In the pattern He has planned.

There is no possible way we can know all the concerns, thoughts, and perhaps even doubts that pass through the mind of people in pain. We have tried to present some of the thoughts we have gleaned from the study of God's word that might be a source of help and strength for some struggling soul.

I have this urging from within to encourage you to become a Christian. The Christian has more with which to fight these struggles than the unbeliever. I sincerely hope you will renounce sin and turn to God and be immersed into Christ, to rise to live the new life of the Christian the rest of your days here, come what will.

God bless you, my friend. I love you.

QUESTIONS FOR CLASS DISCUSSION

1. How is the easiest way of explaining anything that happens to us? What do you think of it?

2. Discuss some of the other possible causes of suffering.

3. If God is all-loving and all-powerful, why does He permit the innocent to suffer?

4. Discuss the idea of unusual suffering because of unusual sin.

5. In what way has God limited Himself as regards human suffering?

5

Abortion and the Christian Conscience

There is no issue more critical to Western Civilization than
the one we are discussing in this chapter. It really is a matter
of life and death to every living person. It affords no place for
neutrality for a single one of us. It is the very heart and soul of
our public ethic. Our resolution of the abortion issue will do
more to define our national agenda and determine our destiny
as a civilization than any other before us.

From the days of our beginning, public acceptance of the
sanctity of human life has been of top priority with us. Histori-
cally, Americans have always held that life is a gift of God. The
very first of the *inalienable rights,* said in the preamble to the
Declaration of Independence to be endowed by our Creator, is
life, then liberty, and the pursuit of happiness. But the *Roe-v-
Wade* decision of the U. S. Supreme Court on January 22,
1973, granting a mother the right to terminate the life of her

unborn child has changed all that. There has been nothing since the Civil War that has divided the nation as much as that arbitrary judicial legislative landmark decision.

In the twenty years that decision has been the law, we have seen the fight move from one battleground to another. Early on, the debate centered around when life begins. If it could have been established that life didn't begin until the second trimester of pregnancy, abortion before that point, would not constitute a killing. However, it is as Gary N. Keener wrote in the *Gospel Advocate,* November 1988,

> A scientific consensus (was) developed, consolidated during congressional hearings in 1981, that life begins with conception and that the fetus is indeed a human being, and it discredited the "potential life" argument as justification for abortion.

Of course it took neither a scientist nor a congressional panel to know that. An old man out in the backwoods of the country, with only an elementary grade education, all dressed up in his bib overalls, chewing on a blade of grass could see through that. His simple observation was, "If it ain't alive, don't kill it."

So for awhile the debate was moved to the question whether the living fetus is a human being and deserves the protection as such under the Constitution. The old backwoodsman helped us through that one, too. "If it ain't human," he asked, "what is it?"

"The real question," then is as President Ronald Reagan wrote in his book, *Abortion and the Conscience of the Nation,* ". . . whether that tiny human life has a God-given right to be protected by the law—the same right we have." Then the President sounded a word of caution. He said,

> The cultural environment for a human holocaust is present whenever any society can be misled into defining individuals as less than human and therefore devoid of value and respect.

Well, the battle lines were redrawn again; this time around the right of a woman to an abortion in the event of a pregnancy resulting from rape or incest or when the pregnancy threatened her own life or health. This seemed to have some merit. At least it had compassion. It had appeal, especially in the religious community. So abortion advocates gained support of some professed Christians.

But that, too, is an obvious diversionary maneuver because we all know that is not why feminists want abortion rights—that only a very small percentage of the one-and-a-half million abortions annually are for reasons of incest and rape—two percent, at the most! Some sources say less than one percent. But if society will approve killing the unborn baby for the hard cases such as these, it is simple to move on to the easy ones.

It's as Richard John Neuhaus, editor of *First Things*, wrote in the December 1991 issue of that magazine: "The license to kill, no matter how carefully crafted at first, cannot be contained. In law, in habits of mind, and in everyday behavior, killing is socially contagious." For that reason, among others, all civilized societies sharply restrict the permissions given for one person to kill another. They do not recognize private agreements for one person to take the life of another in order to serve the interests of one party or both.

Currently, the battle cry is for a woman's right over her own body to abort an unwanted pregnancy at any time and for any reason. It is argued as a legitimate means of birth control, population control, and family planning, simply as an exercise of women's rights. It is used when the woman just simply doesn't want the baby; it would be inconvenient, a hindrance to her career, a financial hardship, the wrong sex, or for whatever cause.

My friend, *we just cannot; we simply must not license any person to kill, or assist in the killing of an innocent human being,* whether preborn or newborn or sick or elderly, for whatever noble purpose may be claimed, because once such license is granted, the practice quickly spreads from the hard cases to the easy and human life becomes cheap.

We have always recognized the limitations of personal rights and liberties. Your First Amendment right of free speech does not give you the right to scream "fire" in a crowded theater—an old illustration, but a good one. Nor does it give you the liberty to speak slanderous things of other people. Freedom of the press does not license citizens to print their own money. No one is ever free to do with his or her own body that which would inflict bodily harm or death upon another person. A man or woman known to be infected with the HIV virus, for example, is not free to knowingly expose another person. A person whose blood alcohol content is more than one-tenth of one percent does not have the right to drive his car. And a woman's rights over her own body must never be considered a license to destroy another life.

The Bible says that "God created man in his own image, in the image of God created he him; male and female created he them. And God blessed them, and God said unto them, Be fruitful, and multiply, and replenish the earth" (Genesis 1:27, 28). God created all the other living creatures too, but He created man in His own image. That makes man extra special. He is different in nature from every other living creature. He is "the offspring of God" (Acts 17:28, 29). Then God pronounced the severest penalty of all on him who sheds the blood of his fellowman. "Whoso sheddeth man's blood, by man shall his blood be shed . . ." He commanded, and He made the reason unmistakably clear, ". . . for in the image of God made he man" (Genesis 9:6).

He is equally as emphatic and plain in the protection of the unborn person. He said,

> If men strive, and hurt a woman with child, so that her fruit depart from her, and yet no mischief follow [the child doesn't die]: he shall be surely punished, according as the woman's husband will lay upon him: and he shall pay as the judges determine; and if any mischief follow [that is, if the child dies], then thou shalt give life for life (Exodus 21:22, 23).

God just does not tolerate the destruction of the unborn child. He has never taken murder lightly. The greatest single indignity or insult a person makes to God is that of murder. Proverbs 6:16, 17 declares that God hates hands that shed innocent blood. Life is the gift of God. "He giveth to all, life, breath and all things" (Acts 17:25). And verse 28 says, "In him we live, and move, and have our being."

The unborn baby, the live fetus if you will, is not merely a "blob of flesh and blood" as the unbeliever argues. More importantly, God considers it a person. He said to Jeremiah, "Before I formed thee in the belly, I knew thee, and before thou camest forth out of the womb, I sanctified thee, and I ordained thee a prophet unto the nations" (Jeremiah 1:5). And David prayed,

> For thou hast possessed my reins: thou has covered me in my mother's womb [thou didst weave me in my mother's womb]. I will praise thee: for I am fearfully and wonderfully made: marvelous are thy works: and that my soul knoweth right well. My substance [body] was not hid from thee, when I was made in secret, and curiously wrought in the lowest parts of the earth. Thine eyes did see my substance [unborn substance, or unborn body], yet being unperfect; and in thy book all my members were written, which in continuance were fashioned, when as yet there was none of them.

This is the Scripture's most complete account of prenatal development. "Thou hast woven me in my mother's womb" is a description of the way God laces the tissues and vessels and sinews together to make a human body. "I am fearfully and wonderfully made," says David. And don't we all! Then he shouts, "I will praise thee!" What a great thought! Indeed, the secret workings of God are marvelous.

It is interesting, too, that in the original language of the New Testament, there is no word to distinguish between the *unborn* and the *newborn* or the young child. For example,

Luke 1:41 tells us that after Mary, the mother of Jesus, learned she was to give birth to the Christ child, she went to visit Elizabeth and Zacharias, the parents of John the Baptist. John had not yet been born, "And it came to pass, that when Elizabeth heard the salutation of Mary, the *babe* leaped in her womb." Notice that this was a *babe*, not a *fetus*.

Then, in the next chapter (2:16), after the angelic chorus had announced the birth of Jesus and gone into heaven, the Scripture says the shepherds "came with haste, and found Mary, and Joseph, and the *babe* lying in a manger." The word for the unborn John the Baptist in Elizabeth's womb is the same word as for the newborn Jesus lying in the manger. My friend, God makes no distinction in the Bible between the unborn baby and the newborn baby or the small child.

With this knowledge, it must be obvious, then, that the mass killing of preborn babies in the American society is no different in the sight of God than the mass killings of newborn babies by the Egyptian Pharaoh in order to control the population of the Israelites (Exodus 1:8-22) or the mass killing of the newborn and small children by Herod in his effort to destroy Jesus as recorded in Matthew 2:16.

There is no biblical justification for abortion on demand. That is an obvious reason for the militant attacks we are witnessing against the Bible as a suitable guide for contemporary living. Abortion on demand is not compatible with the biblical ethic. In order to accept abortion, society must reject the ethic of the Bible and accept the ethic of the humanist, materialist—the unbeliever by whatever name you give him. Those of us who believe the Bible is the inspired word of God and that it is suitable for teaching, for reproof, for correction, and for instruction in righteousness, have every right and responsibility to speak its message loud and clear throughout the land.

Abortion was commonly practiced in the Greek and Roman world when Christianity made its appearance there. But wherever the first century Christians went, they preached Jesus

Christ. And not by political action, not by civil disobedience, but by prayerfully preaching and teaching the good news of the lifestyle of Christ and His salvation, they developed a Christian conscience by which it was said, "They turned the world upside down" (Acts 17:6) and thereby corrected such evils. That's the challenge for today's Christians.

My friend, we must not let this issue become clouded with the charge that it's a political one, and churches and preachers should stay out of it. While the subject has strong political overtones all right, it is basically and essentially a matter of morals and ethics and Christian faith and conscience. There is more involved here than someone's rights; the great concern is of what is right. And it is to these things we have addressed ourselves in this message.

The purpose of this message is twofold: (1) to inject into current discussions on this subject what the key issue really is, the *sanctity of human life*, including that of the preborn; and by doing that (2) to teach and to urge a private conscience that says, despite the legality of abortion for any cause, I will have no part in it, and a public conscience that will not license the killing of an unborn baby as an acceptable solution to the problem of an unwanted pregnancy or a means of birth or population control.

I hope you are a Christian and you are taking a firm stand with God and Christ in protection of innocent human life. But if you're not a Christian, it is my prayer you will lose no time in becoming such. Confess Christ, turn from whatever sin there is in your life in repentance, and be baptized into Christ as you are immersed into His death. Then become involved with Him in the greatest life in this world and enjoy the hope of even a better life in the world to come.

God bless you. I love you, I really do.

QUESTIONS FOR CLASS DISCUSSION

1. How did *Roe v. Wade* reverse the American conscience regarding the sanctity of human life?

2. Discuss the progressiveness in the abortion debate.

3. What is the current focal point in the debate?

4. Discuss the dangers of licensing any person or group of persons to take the life of an innocent person.

5. Why is it biblically wrong to take the life of an innocent person?

6

Do-It-Yourself Death

I Samuel 31:1-6

Now the Philistines fought against Israel: and the men of Israel fled from before the Philistines, and fell down slain in mount Gilboa. And the Philistines followed hard upon Saul and upon his sons; and the Philistines slew Jonathan, and Abinadab, and Melchishua, Saul's sons. And the battle went sore against Saul, and the archers hit him; and he was sore wounded of the archers. Then said Saul unto his armourbearer, Draw thy sword, and thrust me through therewith; lest these uncircumcised come and thrust me through, and abuse me. But his armourbearer would not; for he was sore afraid. Therefore Saul took a sword, and fell upon it. And when his armourbearer saw that Saul was dead, he fell likewise upon his sword, and died with him. So Saul died, and his three sons, and his armourbearer, and all his men, that same day together.

In the course of an average week, we in the *Search* offices will receive from one to any number of telephone calls from people with questions about suicide: "Is it 'the unpardonable sin'?" "Can a person who commits suicide be forgiven?" "Why do people commit suicide?"—and many others, some of which we will try to help with in this study.

Suicide is the eighth leading cause of death in the general population of America—seventh among males and tenth among females. It is the third (some say second) leading cause among the youth, following closely behind drunk driving as number one, and murder as number two. That isn't news to you because that's a widely publicized fact and is the cause of much concern among us.

However, in an article in *The Sunday Oklahoman,* April 28, 1991, staff writer J. E. McReynolds reported that "during the last decade, U.S. suicide rates for those older than sixty-five rose twenty-five percent." According to McReynolds, "Although senior citizens make up only eleven percent of the U.S. population, they accounted for about twenty-five percent of the suicides in 1988." That does come as a surprise because the increased rate of suicide among the senior people has not been widely publicized.

Well, that gives you some idea of the problem confronting us. For a do-it-yourself society, we have called this message "Do-It-Yourself Death."

I want to preface my remarks today by saying that I am not a physician, so this won't be a medical study. Neither am I a psychologist nor a sociologist, so it won't be a psychological or sociological analysis of the problem of suicide. It isn't that such studies aren't interesting or profitable; I have found them so and will be quoting from some of those sources. And I recognize these as invaluable sources of encouragement to troubled people. But I am a gospel (good news) preacher (herald) and, and I believe there is a spiritual dimension to the problem of suicide which those others, as prepared and as competent as they are in their respective fields, cannot address. So along with you, I am going to be examining the Scriptures to see what we can learn from the word of God.

So far as I am able to find, there are only seven occurrences of suicide in the Bible. The first one is in Judges chapter 9. It's the story of Abimelech, a very wicked man with an ego as big as a mountain. His monumental evil and arrogance led to his downfall, and lest it should have been said of him, he was slain by a woman, he commanded his armorbearer to kill him, and he did. That is the tragic end of a pompous and self-important life.

Next is Samson, the strong man, of whom we read in Judges 16. It is a long story that actually begins in chapter 13. He fell in love with a conniving woman who learned the secret of his strength and brought him to shame before his enemies. They put out both his eyes, made sport of him publicly and gave Dagon their god the praise. Samson prayed to God for strength to avenge himself and God gave it. So Samson grasped the two middle pillars on which the house rested and braced himself against them so that the house collapsed on him and on the lords of the Philistines. He chose rather to die at his own hands with his enemies than suffer the disgrace of his captivity resulting from his irreverent life.

The next is that of King Saul in our Scripture reading today in I Samuel 31. When God chose Saul to be the first king of Israel, he was a very humble man. But his success and power "went to his head," as we sometimes say, and he became so proud and evil that God wouldn't even talk to him (I Samuel 28:6). Israel was at war with the Philistines. The battle was going against Israel. Saul's men were in hasty retreat and some of his mighty men had been killed. Defeat appeared certain and King Saul commanded his armorbearer to thrust him through with his sword. But the armorbearer refused to do it. So rather than to be taken captive and suffer torture and humiliation, King Saul took his own life by falling on his sword. So did his armorbearer.

Ahithophel was a wise counsellor to King David who never seemed to err in his advice. But when he joined Absalom's plot against David, Absalom chose not to regard his counsel. His advice was wise; but Hushai advised otherwise. Second Samuel 17:23 says, "When Ahithophel saw that his counsel was not followed, he saddled his donkey and arose and went to his home, to his city, and set his house in order, and strangled [hanged] himself; thus he died and was buried in the grave of his father" (NASV). Such pride!

Then there was Zimri, the fifth sovereign of the kingdom of Israel (after the division). He reigned only seven days. Originally he commanded half the chariots in the royal army, and gained the throne by the murder of King Elah. But the army made Omri king, and Omri marched against Tirzah where Zimri was. And according to I Kings 16:18, 19, when Zimri saw that the city was taken, he went into the citadel of the king's house, and burned it over him. He died in the fire because of his sins which he sinned, doing evil in the sight of the Lord.

And finally, there is Judas Iscariot, one of the Savior's chosen Twelve, who betrayed the Lord for thirty pieces of silver. Then, remorseful over the evil he had done in betraying innocent blood, he was overcome with guilt and shame and went out and hanged himself (Matthew 27:1-5).

Perhaps more important than the mere knowledge of those incidents is an awareness of the help God provides to prevent such a tragedy in our own lives or in the lives of our family and friends. For example, in the newspaper article I mentioned awhile ago, J. E. McReynolds observed that "religion is the one factor that holds people back" or restrains people from taking their own lives. Religious faith contributes to good mental and physical health. It has always been so. Sociologist Steven Stack of Pennsylvania State University is quoted in an article in *U. S. News & World Report* (June 20, 1983) as seeing a relationship between the rising suicide rate among youths and their lagging church attendance. "In his view," the magazine says, "religious beliefs tend to support people through life's trials and lend meaning to suffering."

Why do people take their own lives? Well, according to sociologists one thing seems to be certain—it is not an inherited tendency or trait. More than any single reason, suicides usually result from a combination of factors. The teenager would likely have different reasons for suicide than the elderly. It's evident that we won't have time to mention every cause and contributing factor, even if we knew them all.

But in his book, *What You Should Know About Suicide,* Dr. Bill Blackburn mentions twelve things that motivate people to consider suicide, such things as: to escape an intolerable situation, to punish survivors, to get attention, to join a deceased loved one, to be punished. Blackburn says such a person's "pet sin" may be interpreted by him to be the unpardonable sin so he must be punished. And then some take their lives so as not to be a "burden."

Well, aside from the apparent physical considerations, I believe there are some deep, underlying causes that may be more real but less obvious than those, the main one being the person's outlook on life, which is determined more by his or her thinking about God.

I mean the suicidal person may have a materialistic perspective of life. He may be looking at life as the dictionary defines it, merely as "that period between birth and death." If that's it, and there is nothing more to it than that, I suppose if at any time life became unbearable for any reason, to shorten it by a do-it-yourself end would not only be permissible but advisable. But the believer knows that life is a very precious gift of God. In Acts 17:25 the Scriptures simply say God gives to all life and breath and all things. Believing that, human life, my life, becomes very sacred to me. To take it would be to destroy the most priceless gift God has given me. Simple gratitude, if nothing else, says I should cherish it and protect it and preserve it and be a good steward of it.

The suicidal person may be suffering from low self-esteem. A growing perception of humanity is that we are mere animals. We have been educated that way. From kindergarten to university, we are taught that man is the product of an accidental process called evolution, without any supernatural intervention, just certain chemical and biological forces working together within a long period of time to produce what we are. And if we have that low estimate of ourselves, and life becomes unendurable, there would be no reason for not ending it.

But the believer knows "we are the offspring of God" (Acts 17:28). We are God's children by creation and we bear the image of deity (Genesis 1:26, 27). To take human life, whether my own or someone else's, is the greatest indignity and insult to God there is, and God will hold the murderer accountable, whether it's self-murder or otherwise. You might want to read Genesis 9:5, 6.

Many suicidal people have lost, or have never known, purpose in their lives. To them, life has been only a biological accident anyway, so what's the big deal about ending it? If a person's purpose for living is the accumulation of wealth, and things and life are measured by them, at any time losses become greater than the gain, then life is not worth living. And if, as some believe, pleasure is the chief aim of life, when the pain outweighs the pleasure, life is no longer worth living; terminate it.

But you see, to the person who believes in God and in Christ, there is a more noble purpose in living. He who brought us from our mother's womb called us with a holy calling to make a difference in the world and to glorify Him by doing it. "We are workers together with God" (II Corinthians 6:1). We are God's offspring, doing God's work and fulfilling His purposes in our lives. So suicide is not an alternative for the Christian. He doesn't even consider it.

Whether it is pain or poverty or pressures, or whatever it is that seems so unbearable as to cause a person to consider suicide as an escape from it all, the believer can be assured that God is, that He loves us, knows all about it, and will never, never forsake us. The writer of the book of Hebrews seized upon this promise to say,

> Let your way of life be free from the love of money, being content with what you have; for He Himself has said, I will never desert you, nor will I ever forsake you, so that we confidently say, "The Lord is my helper, I will not be afraid (Hebrews 13:5, NASV).

The apostle Paul found God's grace sufficient to sustain him through the sufferings of his "thorn in the flesh" (II Corinthians 13:10).

Do you know Him, my friend? You can come to Him through a trusting faith in Christ, repentance from your past sinful lifestyle, and obedience to Him in baptism for the forgiveness of your sins through His shed blood (Revelation 1:5; Romans 6:3, 4). I hope you will.

In the book I mentioned earlier, *What You Should Know About Suicide,* Dr. Blackburn advises anyone thinking about suicide to first ask himself two questions: "Who will find my body?" and "What effect will my death have on those closest to me?" These are worthy questions.

When trying to determine whether a person is suicidal, Dr. Keith McKee, a member of the Edmond Church and director of the Edmond Guidance Clinic looks for "the three *h*'s" as he calls them: *hopelessness, helplessness,* and *haplessness.* "Hopelessness," he says, "is when the person doesn't see any alternative; helplessness is that he is helpless to do anything; and haplessness is when the patient is unable to respond" (*Edmond Evening Sun,* April 12, 1989).

There is a lot about this subject we haven't discussed, and there is a lot more that needs to be said. I pray you have been blessed.

God bless you. I love you.

QUESTIONS FOR CLASS DISCUSSION

1. What are some of the psychological explanations for suicide?

2. What are some of the more deep-seated reasons for suicide?

3. Discuss some of the instances of suicide in the Scriptures.

4. What is the correlation between church attendance and suicide?

5. What is the most effective resistant to suicide?

7

Euthanasia

I Samuel 31:1-6

Now the Philistines fought against Israel: and the men of Israel fled from before the Philistines, and fell down slain in mount Gilboa. And the Philistines followed hard upon Saul and upon his sons; and the Philistines slew Jonathan, and Abinadab, and Melchishua, Saul's sons. And the battle went sore against Saul, and the archers hit him; and he was sore wounded of the archers. Then said Saul unto his armourbearer, Draw thy sword, and thrust me through therewith; lest these uncircumcised come and thrust me through, and abuse me. But his armourbearer would not; for he was sore afraid. Therefore Saul took a sword, and fell upon it. And when his armourbearer saw that Saul was dead, he fell likewise upon his sword, and died with him. So Saul died, and his three sons, and his armourbearer, and all his men, that same day together.

Paul Kurtz, leading humanist in America, says in his book, *Forbidden Fruit,* that "every culture needs an established set of moral principles and values to live by." We couldn't agree with him more on that statement. Where we disagree with him is that we believe that Jesus Christ introduced the highest and noblest set of principles and values to be found anywhere. We believe our Western society and culture, and American society in particular, made a mistake when we renounced that way. Churches of Christ are a people of "restoration," a restoration of that faith and that way revealed to us in the New Testament. And that's what we're doing here. We're searching the word of God for His way to live this life and to prepare for the next world.

Euthanasia, or assisted suicide, has thrust itself on the public conscience in several ways in the fairly recent past. There was the unexpected and phenomenal sale of Derek Humphry's book, *Final Exit*. It's reported to have sold in excess of 300,000 copies right off.

But probably the greatest is the work of Dr. Kevorkian and his "mercitron" machine, as he calls it, or "death machine" as it's called by others. And then there was the referendum put before the people of Washington State in an election late in 1991 that had to do with some aspects of the subject of euthanasia. All of that has forced the subject of "easy death," and "death with dignity," and "living wills," and all of that into our conversation and conscience a lot.

It's quite a marvelous age in which we are living, isn't it? It's certainly no mistake to say that electricity, the automobile, the telephone, television, air-travel, computers, fax machines, organ transplants, laser surgery, pace makers, respirators, life support systems and, well, a whole host of other new inventions, discoveries, techniques, methods, and practices have literally revolutionized man's life on the earth.

Not many of us have had to live in a world without all these things and it is highly improbable that we would want to do it. But then, life was much more simple without them. Along with all that technology came a lot of very complicated problems, too. Along with these machines and technology for saving our lives or extending our lives or improving on the quality of life, such things as what we call "life supports," for example, come a lot of complex questions about their ethical use—when it is right to use them, and when it isn't.

And the questions have come upon us so suddenly that we really have not found answers to them yet. We are still struggling with them. And while we struggle, real people like us are being forced into these life-and-death situations. Out of it all come questions about when—if ever—is it right to destroy the unborn infant, or what about refusing nourishment to the newborn, the deformed infant, so as to let him die in infancy, or what about an "easy death" or euthanasia for the terminally ill, or death by assistance for the person just tired of living or people who just want to hasten the process of dying? Well, there is a lot being said and written about "planned death," "death with dignity," "living wills" and all of that sort of thing.

Often Christians feel that these are social problems, unrelated to the gospel, and that the church and preachers should busy themselves with preaching the gospel and leave these questions to other people. It is because that attitude has prevailed so strongly that solutions to these real-life situations are sought almost totally independent of the Christian influence and the influence of the Bible. And really, these are social challenges to the gospel of Jesus Christ. Euthanasia is a moral question of immense magnitude.

If I were a physician, you would expect me to speak about the medical ethics of all of this, the Hippocratic Oath perhaps, and the role of the physician in all of it. If I were an attorney or a politician, I would be expected to address the legal aspects of legislation; or if I were a sociologist, I would study the impact it might have on families or society in general if we were to accept euthanasia either legally or socially. And since I am a minister of the gospel, you are expecting me to present some biblical or spiritual guidance.

Well, advocates of euthanasia say the Bible is neutral on suicide or euthanasia either one. But it isn't so. Perhaps the best known instance of suicide in the Bible is the passage which we read at the outset of this program today found in the last chapter of the Old Testament book of I Samuel and the first chapter of II Samuel. King Saul, wounded by the archers of the armies of the enemy, asked his armorbearer to use his sword to put him out of his misery. The armorbearer, knowing how serious the deed would be, refused to do that. So Saul took his own life.

Later an Amalekite passed by the battle field and saw that Saul was dead along with his sons, and so he went to David, who was to be the next king of Israel, and he claimed that seeing the suffering Saul there, he had "compassion" on him and put him out of his misery. He really thought David would reward him for his love and compassion for Israel's king who was suffering so. But instead, David called him to account. Since the Amalekite had lived in Israel for a long time, David said, he surely understood the laws of that people. To kill the king, even out of compassion, was utterly unacceptable and David had the Amalekite taken out and killed for his presumption against Saul and against human life.

Now in spite of the denials of the proponents of euthanasia, it is a moral issue. And the two greatest moral statements known to the human race are the Ten Commandments of the Old Testament and Christ's Sermon on the Mount in the New Testament, both of which unequivocally forbid the destruction of innocent human life. It is an absurd contradiction to think of trying to arrive at a practical conclusion in our current debate on these matters without considering these two moral documents.

The Sixth Commandment of the Old Testament simply says, "Thou shalt not kill," or more accurately, "Thou shalt not do murder." The Son of God goes even further to denounce evil in the heart that would prompt such a killing. From the biblical perspective then, it is always wrong to directly intend to terminate an innocent human life. Without any doubt, killing another person constitutes the greatest possible insult to God. The reason is that God made man in His own image.

So euthanasia is also a question of, well, not the *quality of life*, but the *sanctity* of human life. All human life is different from animal life that roams the woods and the plains. Whether it is preborn or newborn or aged, we are not animals; we are "the offspring of God" (Acts 17:28), and we bear His image (Genesis 1:27). King David of Israel wrote in the Eighth Psalm:

When I consider thy heavens, the work of thy fingers, the moon and the stars, which thou hast ordained; what is man, that thou art mindful of him? or the son of man, that thou visitest him? For thou hast made him a little lower than the angels [literally, a little lower than God], and hast crowned him with glory and honor.

Now any teaching that presents a lower view of the life of man is the very root cause of the current state of man's inhumanity to man.

Francis Shaeffer, in *What Ever Happened To The Human Race?* says:

Putting pressure on the public and on legislators to accept a lower view of the human beings, small groups of people often argue their case using a few extreme examples to gain sympathy for ideas and practices that later are not limited to extreme cases. These then become the common practice of the day.

Well, abortion is a good example of that. It was argued in cases of rape and incest and has now become a commonly accepted practice of birth and population control, merely the free exercise of a woman's rights.

And Richard John Neuhaus, editor of *First Things*, writes in the December 1991 issue of that magazine, saying that

... the purveyors of hemlock claim that the legal changes they propose are carefully crafted to address the hard cases of those who have been called "the biologically persistent"—those who go on living after they have lost their "quality of life" and are therefore, as we are told, dead. We know from hard experience, however, that the license to kill, no matter how carefully crafted it is at first, cannot be contained. In law, in the hearts of mind, and in everyday behavior, killing is socially contagious.

In his book, *Abortion and the Conscience of the Nation*, President Ronald Reagan rightly observed, "We cannot diminish the value of one category of human life—the unborn—without diminishing the value of all human life." And so, in so short a time, we have seen the battle move swiftly from abortion to infanticide to euthanasia, from the killing of the unwanted unborn, to the unwanted newborn, to the unwanted sick and elderly.

Malcom Muggeridge wrote in the *Humane Holocaust,* "Euthanasia, it is true, has not yet been legalized except in some American states, but notoriously it is being practiced on an ever-increasing scale." It's interesting: "The first direct order for euthanasia came from Adolph Hitler in 1939." And Muggeridge says,

> Surely some future Gibbon [or historian] surveying our times will note sardonically that it took no more than three decades to transform a war crime into an act of compassion, thereby enabling the victors in the war against Nazi-ism to adopt the very practices for which the Nazis had been solemnly condemned at Nuremberg. Then they could mount their own humane holocaust, which in its range and in the number of its victims may soon far surpass the Nazi one.

My friend, euthanasia—easy death, death with dignity, assisted suicide, mercy killing, whatever name you give it—is not of God but of evil.

The Bible says that life is the gift of God, that God gives to all life, and breath, and all things (Acts 17:25). And the next verse teaches that that is universally true of all. Humanity is made of one blood, all nations of men for to dwell upon the face of the earth regardless of color, or sex, or age, preborn, newborn, and all the rest of us, then also have received the gift of life from Him. To take the life of an innocent human being is to deprive that person, whether it's oneself or another, of the gift that only God can give.

The Christian believes that the body in which he lives throughout his earthly sojourn is not his alone, but God's. The Scriptures say,

> Know ye not that your body is the temple of the Holy Spirit which is in you, which ye have of God, and ye are

not your own? Ye are bought with a price: therefore glorify God in your body, and in your spirit, which are God's (I Corinthians 6:19, 20).

Dr. Batsell Barrett Baxter, who for many years was the speaker on the Herald of Truth radio and television program, was persuaded in the last days of his life to write an autobiography. He called it *Every Life A Plan of God,* and in the very first paragraph he said,

> In a very real sense, every person created by God has a place in His ultimate plan and each of us, as a creature possessing freedom of will, either facilitates or frustrates God's plan for his life.

To take into our own hands, to plan the time and the circumstances of our own death, or to assist another in doing so, in spite of all of the good intentions is but to frustrate God's plan for a human life and is therefore an affront to God. None of us can know the day of our death. Of course not. No one of us can know what the world has in store for us, whether weal or woe, pain or pleasure, but we need have no fear of pain beyond the grave. Most of us are willing to linger here and wait for the sunset, if it means even another fifty years. Dying is dreaded. Of course it is. I'm sure it isn't an easy experience even at its very best. But neither was being born easy. It was a frightening experience that opened up a whole new world of living. And so it is with dying. The dread and fear of dying is diminished greatly by our faith in the crucified and resurrected Christ and by living and dying as a Christian.

I hope you are a Christian right now, but if you are not, why wait until your death bed to try to become so. Why not put your trust and hope in Jesus Christ right now? Why not abandon the sinful lifestyle that has characterized your past and be immersed into the death of Jesus, buried with Him in baptism, and begin living for Him and for eternity today?

I suppose the most attractive appeal made by the advocates of euthanasia is the appeal to the exercise of personal choice.

Humanist Manifesto II says on page 19,

> To enhance freedom and dignity the individual must experience a full range of civil liberties in all societies. . . . That includes a recognition of an individual's right to die with dignity, euthanasia, and the right to suicide.

But wait a minute. A freedom that can legally and morally be given away is very fragile and conditional and really isn't freedom at all. To allow another person to kill us is not the exercise of freedom but the most radical relinquishment of freedom imaginable. In such a case, a person's life is no longer his, but it belongs to the person or the persons into whose power he gives it. No advocate of civil liberties and the right to self-determination should ever want to see that possibility made available.

Let me quickly review, then we'll close. We've said,

(1) The other side of the euthanasia question is the biblical one.

(2) Euthanasia is a moral issue and cannot be settled apart from the two greatest statements on morals and ethics the world has ever known, The Ten Commandments of the Old Testament and Christ's Sermon on the Mount, both of which enunciate clearly that it is wrong to take the life of an innocent person under any circumstances.

(3) Euthanasia is a question of the *sanctity* of life, *not the quality* of life. Human life is sacred because man is the offspring of God, and because life is the gift of God.

(4) Euthanasia frustrates the plan of God for a person's life.

(5) Euthanasia is not of God, but of evil.

(6) The Christian's concern is not *rights* but *right.*

I guess it all comes down to this: either God is the creator of the whole man, or He is creator of none. Either He is the ruler of the whole world, or He is ruler of none. If He is only going to be God of the things that fit conveniently into the corners of my life, only to be displaced by something else that might decorate that corner more attractively at times, then He is not much of a God. My world view is determined by my faith in God, what I believe about Him.

May God bless you. I do love you.

QUESTIONS FOR CLASS DISCUSSION

1. Relate the events leading up to the death of King Saul.

2. Show how the Bible is not neutral regarding euthanasia.

3. Why should a society never license anyone to take the life of another innocent person?

4. Why are we talking about taking the life of an "innocent" person?

5. What is the greatest insult man can make to God? Why is it so?

8

Is There Life After Death?

Job 14:14

If a man die, shall he live again? all the days of my appointed time will I wait, till my change come.

"Is there life after death?" That question is as old as man himself. Yet, it is as timely as this morning's newspaper. Philosophers, sages, scientists all, have devoted themselves over the millenniums of human existence to find a suitable answer. And today there will be thousands of common ordinary people like you and me standing by the open grave at the burial of a loved one or friend who will roll it over and over in their own minds, "Is this the end of all, or is there life after death?" What do you think?

Some of the very oldest documents in existence evidence man's belief in life after death. The book of Job, for example, is among some of the earliest known writings and bears the question, "If a man die, shall he live again" (Job 14:14)? And in the enlightened and sophisticated society of the twentieth century, so strongly influenced by science and secularism, more than those concerning the national economy or debt or health care is the question, "Is there life after death?" It won't go away.

So what does science have to offer by way of an answer to

this persistent problem? Not much—well, nothing would be more accurate because, you see, it's a question beyond the scientific domain. As much as we have come to appreciate science and to rely on it to improve the quality of our lives and to extend them here for a few more years, there are some things beyond its sphere. Science does not deal in morals, values, or purposes. Life after death is not something that can be observed, repeated, and investigated in the laboratory; therefore, it is beyond the scientific method to answer pro or con about life beyond the grave.

Western society's pervading philosophy is humanism, which is all bound up in the theory of evolution—that this world and all there is in it is the product of mere chance; that man evolved from the lower species of life and is, therefore, wholly matter. If we ask the humanist then, "Is there life after death?" the answer is flatly, "No!" On page 17, *Humanist Manifesto II* says simply, "There is no credible evidence that life survives the death of the body."

If modern science and philosophy are unable to provide a suitable answer to this momentous question, to whom can we turn? Religion, perhaps?

Well, it goes without saying that the idea of life after death is the touchstone of all world religions. Some Eastern religions—Hinduism and Buddhism, specifically—solve the problem with reincarnation. Islam holds that the dead remain in their graves until the end of the world, at which time everyone will assemble before Allah for the final judgment. And although the idea of afterlife isn't as dominant and clear in Judaism as in Christianity, the doctrine has been, and still is among the more orthodox, central to Jewish faith.

Life after death was one of the cardinal doctrines of New Testament Christianity. However, according to an article by Kenneth L. Woodward in the March 27, 1989 issue of *Newsweek* magazine, it isn't so with much of modern Christianity. Woodward interviewed a cross-section of accepted theologians and widely acclaimed authors, only to find that

Easter Sunday is the one Sunday in the year when
Christians can anticipate a sermon about life after death.
But out of principle, many Christian clergy are loath to
mention heaven—or, for that matter, hell. For some
pastors it's a question of rhetorical modesty: after centuries of cajoling listeners with overly graphic sermons on
the pleasures of heaven and the horrors of hell, preachers today are hesitant to describe places that no one has
actually seen.

According to Douglas Stuart, an evangelical theologian at
Gordon-Conwell Theological Seminary in South Hamilton,
Massachusetts, whom Woodward quotes in his article, "For
others, the problem is that the (mainstream Protestant) clergy
simply don't believe in the afterlife themselves, either the Biblical view or any view."

It is not only true in mainstream Protestant churches but in
Catholic, liberal, conservative, evangelical, and fundamentalist
churches too. According to liberal theologian Max Stackhouse
at Andover-Newton Theological School (as he is quoted in the
Newsweek article), "The prevailing opinion is that when you
die you're dead but God still cares." Rabbi Terry Bard, director
of pastoral services at Boston's Beth Israel Hospital, is quoted
to "sum up the views of many Jews." He says, "Dead is dead,
and what lives on are the children and a legacy of good works."

Well, it must be obvious by now that if it were left to wise
and learned men, the best we could hope for is the reincarnation of Hinduism and Buddhism or New Age religion—a re-
birth again and again in an earthly form here on the earth. But
what does the Bible say? There are still millions of people who
look to it for the answers. We, too, believe the Bible is God's
word and that in it God speaks loud and clear on the question
of life after death.

As sort of an introduction, let's take a quick look at two
statements made by Christ Himself. In Matthew 12 some of
Jesus' critics accused Him of doing His miracles by the power
of Beelzebub, prince of the devils. And in verse 32 He said,

Whosoever speaketh a word against the Son of man, it
shall be forgiven him: but whosoever speaketh against
the Holy Ghost, it shall not be forgiven him, neither in
this world, *neither in the world to come.*

On another occasion Jesus had told his disciples, "It is
easier for a camel to go through the eye of a needle, than for a
rich man to enter into the kingdom of God," and they
were—well, the Bible says—"they were astonished out of measure," and talked among themselves, "Who then can be saved?"
If the rich can't be saved, who on earth can be? So Peter,
impetuous Peter, speaking for the group, said, "Lo, we have
left all, and have followed thee." Jesus answered,

There is no man that hath left house or brethren, or
sisters, or father, or mother, or wife, or children, or
lands, for my sake and the gospel's, but he shall receive
an hundredfold now in *this time . . .* and *in the world to
come* eternal life.

Jesus seems to just assume their belief in "the world to come"
in both of these instances, wouldn't you say?

We have the same teaching in the writings of the Holy
Spirit. For example in Ephesians 1:21, through the apostle
Paul, He speaks of the exaltation of Christ "far above all
principality, and power, and might, and dominion, and every
name that is named, not only in *this world,* but also in *that
[world] which is to come.*" And in I Timothy 4:8 He says,
"Bodily exercise profiteth little: but godliness is profitable unto
all things, having promise of *the life that now is,* and *of that
[life] which is to come.*" And in his great resurrection sermon
in I Corinthians 15, Paul declares, "If in *this life only* we have
hope in Christ, we are of all men most miserable" (verse 19).
Would we be doing the Scriptures injustice to say that the *life
which is to come,* of which the Holy Spirit speaks, is in *the
world which is to come* mentioned by Jesus during His personal ministry?

Of course that devastates the idea of reincarnation, but

then, the Scriptures teach *resurrection,* not reincarnation. Jesus taught *resurrection,* not reincarnation, in Matthew 22:31 and the parallel passages in Mark and Luke. He promised an hour when "all that are in the graves shall hear his voice, And shall come forth; they that have done good, unto the resurrection of life," He said, "and they that have done evil, unto the resurrection of damnation" (John 5:25, 26).

The apostles and other early Christians taught resurrection, even when it meant severest persecution. When Peter and John had healed a lame man at the beautiful gate of the temple and preached that it was in Jesus' name the miracle was done, the priests, the captain of the temple, and the Sadducees came upon them,

> . . . being grieved that they taught the people, and preached through Jesus the resurrection of the dead. And they laid hands on them, and put them in hold [arrested them and later commanded them to cease such preaching] (Acts 3, 4).

When making his defense before the Jewish council, Paul declared, "Of the hope of the resurrection of the dead I am called in question" (Acts 23:1-6). And in his defense before Governor Felix, he said it again:

> But this I confess unto thee that after the way which they [his accusers] call heresy, so worship I the God of my fathers, believing all things which are written in the law and in the prophets; and have hope toward God, which they themselves also allow, that there shall be a resurrection of the dead, both of the just and the unjust (Acts 24:14, 15).

Faith in a resurrection of the just and the unjust, as Paul said, or as Jesus said it in John 5:29, the good and the evil, is founded on the resurrection of Christ. So Paul argues in I Corinthians 15: How can some of you say there is no resurrection? If there is no resurrection Christ has not been raised. But if Christ is raised, it must follow that there is a resurrection.

Faith in the resurrection is a cardinal principle in the process of becoming a Christian. It gives beauty and meaning to baptism. With reference to the great flood, Peter declared,

> Corresponding to that, baptism now saves you—not the removal of dirt from the flesh, but an appeal to God for a good conscience—*through the resurrection of Jesus Christ* (I Peter 3:21, NASV).

And Paul contends that there is really no valid reason for being baptized, if there is no resurrection (I Corinthians 15:29). Of course, he is right.

Is there life beyond the grave? You can be sure of it, my friend. In Hebrews 9:27 the Bible plainly states that "it is appointed unto men once to die, but after this the judgment." Now notice three things in that verse:

(1) It is appointed to men to die. You would believe that if you read it in a comic strip, wouldn't you? Then you can just as readily believe the rest of the verse.

(2) It is appointed to men to die only once. No one has ever proved that to be wrong.

(3) After death there is judgment, a day of reckoning, both for the just and the unjust. So there is death, after that there is the resurrection, and judgment.

So far as a person's destiny in the world to come, there are two possibilities. One is *Heaven;* the other is *Hell.* The word *heaven* appears 582 times in the King James Bible, 327 times in the Old Testament and 255 times in the New. If a person believes the Bible and respects its teachings, he believes in Heaven. Any preaching or system of teaching that denies the hope of Heaven denies the credibility of the Bible and reduces man to the level of beasts and birds.

Hell in the King James Version translates four words; *Sheol* which generally means "the unseen world," but sometimes means "grave"; *Hades* which is the Greek equivalent of "Sheol"; *Tartarus* which is found only in II Peter 2:4 and refs to a place where the wicked dead are imprisoned awaiting judgment; and *Gehenna* which appears most often and refers to a place of eternal punishment of the wicked." Jesus used the word *Gehenna* eleven times and spoke of it as the eternal abode of the wicked and unjust. If a person believes in Jesus Christ, he must believe in the reality of Hell.

Well now, what about it? Where will you spend your eternity? Christ came and died that you might be reconciled to God in Heaven. He "brought life and immortality to light" for us all (II Timothy 1:10), but we each have a choice. I hope you will obey Christ and become a Christian at once.

My friend, it's interesting that in spite of the denial of life after death by many theologians and clergymen—and women—according to a Gallup Poll taken for *Newsweek,* seventy-seven percent of the people believe there is a Heaven and seventy-six percent think they have a good or excellent chance of getting there. And about Hell: fifty-eight percent say they believe there is a Hell and six percent think they have a good or excellent chance of getting there. So despite the vacillating ministry in some churches, most Americans still believe there is life after death, just as the Bible says.

But for those honest souls who are still looking for assurance that being human has more than transitory significance, most American pulpits are of little help. When preachers stop talking about Hell, Heaven won't be far behind. How long has it been since you heard a sermon in your church about Hell? About Heaven? The world needs the gospel—the death of Christ for our sins according to the Scriptures, His burial, and His resurrection according to the Scriptures (I Corinthians 15:4). "After that in the wisdom of God the world by wisdom knew not God, it pleased God by the foolishness of preaching [the death, burial and resurrection of Christ] to save them that believe" (I Corinthians 1:21).

Death awaits us all. Then there is resurrection and judgment, and following the judgment is either Heaven or Hell. You determine your destiny by either accepting or rejecting

Christ and His teachings. Be a Christian, my friend. I pray you will.

May God bless you. I love you.

QUESTIONS FOR CLASS DISCUSSION

1. Show the relevancy of this discussion of life after death.

2. Why can't we turn to science for an answer?

3. What is reincarnation? Why is it not the answer to the question of life after death?

4. Discuss the teachings of Jesus about another life and another world.

5. Show how faith in the resurrection of Jesus Christ is the basis of becoming a Christian and how it enables a person to live faithfully until death.

9

The Resurrection

I Corinthians 15:20-26

But now is Christ risen from the dead, and become the firstfruits of them that slept. For since by man came death, by man came also the resurrection of the dead. For as in Adam all die, even so in Christ shall all be made alive. But every man in his own order: Christ the firstfruits; afterward they that are Christ's at his coming. Then cometh the end, when he shall have delivered up the kingdom to God, even the Father; when he shall have put down all rule and all authority and power. For he must reign, till he hath put all enemies under his feet. The last enemy that shall be destroyed is death.

Nothing is more a part of living than dying. Every day we read about people dying by the thousands from starvation in Ethiopia; from earthquakes in places like Chile, Turkey, Greece, India, and Armenia; in airplane crashes; and from violence in war-torn areas of the world. And we develop a rather philosophical attitude toward death and dying. We accept it somewhat as a necessity on a planet which would otherwise be overpopulated and overcrowded very quickly if people didn't die.

Then one day death becomes much more real and personal. It may be our very own grandmother or mother or our own child, and suddenly death has become, well at best, a puzzle, perhaps a threat, or possibly a terrible injustice. Some have even been known to renounce their faith in God over the death of a loved one. It is difficult to see our own death as a natural phenomenon. Whatever may be our thinking about it, we all know it is inevitable. No one can escape it. It is a necessity for all. There are many mysteries—lots of unknowns.

From as far back as we can know about man, he has wanted to believe there is life beyond the grave and has expressed that desire in many ways: his burial practices, his literature, his music, and yes, even in the way he worships. Is there life beyond the grave? Will our body be resurrected? What kind of body will it be? What hope of a resurrection do we have? And why?

We are not going to search for a philosophical, scientific, or psychological response to the question of resurrection. Some might think it would add "authenticity" to have a panel of athletes, movie stars, and dignitaries, or perhaps some psychiatrists and psychologists tell us about near-death experiences and what they reveal, but when we had finished, we would be back to where we began—the mere conjectures of men. So we are going to simply study the word of God for help on the question of resurrection.

I have been reading some of the popular books available about death and dying. Some are very good. I have been profited by reading a few of them, but they don't really offer anything substantial so far as the question of resurrection is concerned. God has something to say about the subject in the Scriptures, and He deserves to be heard. As a matter of fact, apart from the Scriptures, there is nothing you can confidently "latch on to," or "grab hold of"—nothing upon which a person can build a firm faith or solid hope for a resurrection and life beyond. Yes, the doctrine of a bodily resurrection is a fundamental doctrine of the religion of Christ.

The finest and most thorough dissertation to be found anywhere on the subject is in I Corinthians, chapter 15. It isn't all God has to say on the subject, but it answers a lot of our questions.

As we look at this chapter, please keep in mind that while a resurrection of the body wasn't a strange doctrine to the Jews, the Greek mind found the prospect not only grotesque, but absurd. So it isn't surprising some of the Corinthian Christians were having problems with the idea. Remember too, Paul doesn't address the question of life after death in this chapter. He only examines the idea of resurrection. The other would necessarily follow.

In verses 1 through 11, he establishes his whole argument for a resurrection of the body upon the fact of the resurrection of Christ. He speaks of that doctrine as an essential doctrine in the Christian faith. He offers abundant proof of our Lord's resurrection. He says,

> Moreover, brethren, I declare unto you the gospel which I preached unto you, which also ye have received, and wherein ye stand; by which also ye are saved, if ye keep in memory what I preached unto you, unless ye have believed in vain. For I delivered unto you that which I also received, how that Christ died for our sins according to the scriptures; and that he was buried, and that he rose again the third day according to the scriptures.

Notice how he uses the Scriptures (that would be the Old Testament, of course) as authoritative proof of Christ's resurrection! He points to the empty tomb as further evidence, and if any would be skeptical even yet, he produces more than five hundred eyewitnesses, many of whom were still living, and some of whom he calls by name! Christ had not merely swooned! "He died for our sins." If He weren't alive again, if His resurrection is merely an illusion or delusion or hallucination, then go to the grave where He was buried and produce the body! I love the absolute certainty with which Paul says, "He rose again the third day!"

In verses 12 through 16, Paul writes:

> Now if Christ be preached that he rose from the dead, how say some among you that there is no resurrection? But if there be no resurrection of the dead, then is Christ not risen; and if Christ be not risen, then is our preach-

ing vain, and your faith is also vain. Yea, and we are
found false witnesses of God; because we have testified
of God that he raised up Christ; whom he raised not up,
if so be that the dead rise not. For if the dead rise not,
then is not Christ raised.

Well, one just doesn't escape the force of his logic, does he? It is
just as true today as it was the day he wrote it! Just as surely
as Christ was raised, and the evidence of it is too overwhelming
to pass over or deny, then there has to be a resurrection.

Now, verses 20 through 23:

But now is Christ risen from the dead, and become the
first fruits of them that slept. For since by man came
death, by man came also the resurrection of the dead.
For as in Adam all die, even so in Christ shall all be made
alive. But every man in his own order; Christ the
firstfruits; afterward they that are Christ's at his coming.

Is there going to be a resurrection of the dead to live again?
Oh yes, there is! When will it be? It will be when Jesus Christ
comes again! That will be the end of the world! Paul doesn't
discuss the resurrection of the unbeliever, but they will be
raised at the same time. Jesus said that in John 5:28, 29:

The hour is coming in which all that are in the graves
shall hear his voice, and shall come forth; they that have
done good, unto the resurrection of life; and they that
have done evil, unto the resurrection of damnation.

The good and the bad, the believer and the unbeliever will be
resurrected to live on—somewhere—when Christ returns. We
will discuss that somewhere in other messages in this series.

In verses 29 through 34, we are given some practical appli-
cations of the doctrine of the resurrection.

First, faith in the resurrection gives meaning to a person's
baptism. "Else what shall they do which are baptized for the
dead, if the dead rise not at all? Why are they then baptized for
the dead?" Verses 35 through 49 teach us beyond doubt that

that which is dead and buried and is to be raised again is the natural body. (We will get to that in a moment.) But Paul says, why are we baptized in view of the resurrection of these dead bodies, if they aren't going to be raised?

Next, faith in the resurrection gives meaning to devotion to God and sacrifice in His service. All this Christianity business is not madness if we are to be resurrected to life eternal! "If after the manner of men I have fought with beasts at Ephesus," he asks, "what advantageth it me, if the dead rise not?" He had said in verse 19, "If in this life only we have hope in Christ, we are of all men most miserable."

Third, faith in a resurrection renders sensualism folly. "Let us eat and drink; for tomorrow we die" doesn't sound all that smart when a person considers the fact of a resurrection unto judgment, now does it?

And, in view of a resurrection, association with doubters and skeptics is perilous to the soul. "Be not deceived," he reasons in verse 33, "evil companions corrupt good morals." What a person believes makes a difference in the way he lives. If you want to maintain your faith and hope, don't associate with the profligate and profane, the disbelievers and doubters. That makes sense, doesn't it?

Verses 35 through 49 answer a question very likely in your mind. Paul anticipated it long ago. "How are the dead raised up? And with what body do they come?" He is going to answer it for you, so listen to what he says:

> That which thou sowest is not quickened [made alive], except it die; and that which thou sowest, thou sowest not that body that shall be, but bare grain, it may chance of wheat, or of some other grain; but God giveth it a body as it hath pleased him, and to every seed his own body.

Wheat farmers don't sow the same thing that comes up. They sow a small yellow or brown kernel of grain. But when it breaks through the ground, it is green and in the form of a stalk. That's the way it is with the body and its resurrection. That shouldn't seem so strange, because there are different kinds of bodies. There is one kind for fish, another for beasts, another for birds, and another for man. There are also celestial bodies and bodies terrestrial; and they are all different in appearance. "So also is the resurrection of the dead." The body which is planted in the grave is a corruptible, weak, and sickly one. But it is raised in glory and honor and power! You see, there is a natural body and there is a spiritual body, and as we have born the natural, we must also bear the spiritual. The body we bury in the grave is a natural body, but the body that is to be raised will be a spiritual, glorious one. For, you see, flesh and blood cannot inherit the kingdom of God; neither does corruption inherit incorruption.

Now we come to verse 51, and what a great way to end such a marvelously enlightening and inspiring message on the resurrection: "Behold, I show you a mystery; we shall not all sleep, but we shall all be changed." Some of us will not have died; some will still be living, but we will all be changed, "in a moment, in the twinkling of an eye, at the last trump; for the trumpet shall sound, and the dead shall be raised incorruptible, and we shall be changed."

Death is a necessity, a certainty you cannot possibly avoid or escape. But for the Christian, resurrection is victory! What a powerful statement: "Death is swallowed up in victory. O death, where is thy sting? O grave, where is thy victory?" Let us give thanks to God who gives us the victory over death and the grave through our Lord Jesus Christ!

And the grand conclusion is in verse 58:

> Therefore, my beloved brethren, be ye steadfast, unmovable, always abounding in the work of the Lord, forasmuch as ye know that your labor is not in vain in the Lord.

The disciple of Jesus Christ cannot afford to even consider giving up, falling away, or quitting. He must not permit himself to be discouraged by the world or allured by its attractions. At all costs, he must remain steadfast, unwavering, unfailing, and firm in his faith. There is too much at stake to grow indolent, lazy, or idle in the work of the Lord. There can be no substitute for the victory over death and the grave.

This masterpiece on resurrection in I Corinthians 15 was addressed to Christians, so the unsaved are not mentioned. However, I feel compelled to urge the unsaved to become sharers of this hope and victory by becoming Christians. Surely you believe in Jesus Christ, else you would not still be with me. Confess Him (Romans 10:9, 10), turn from your sinful lifestyle in repentance (Acts 17:30), and be baptized into Jesus Christ to wash away your sins (Acts 22:16) in the blood of Jesus (Revelation 1:5).

God bless you. I love you.

QUESTIONS FOR CLASS DISCUSSION

1. In Paul's great dissertation on the resurrection, on what does he build his case for a general resurrection of the dead?

2. What proof does he offer for it? What do you think of its validity?

3. If the dead are raised, with what body do they come forth? Now explain the greatly controverted verse 29 about being baptized for the dead.

4. Show four ways faith in the resurrection is applicable to Christian living.

5. Discuss the Christian's victory!

STATEMENT   TERMS   DATE

DATE	DESCRIPTION		AMOUNT
	PREVIOUS BALANCE		
8-16-94	Life, Death and Beyond		6.40
	[+ ship/handling]		1.10
			7.50
	Mack Lyon		
	P O Box 371		Pd
	Edmond Ok		9-7-94
	73083		

PREVIOUS BAL.	CHARGES	PAYMENTS	NEW BALANCE
	7.50		

MACK LYON

10

Where are the Dead?

II Corinthians 12:1-5

It is not expedient for me doubtless to glory. I will come to visions and revelations of the Lord. I knew a man in Christ above fourteen years ago, (whether in the body, I cannot tell; or whether out of the body, I cannot tell: God knoweth;) such an one caught up to the third heaven. And I knew such a man, (whether in the body, or out of the body, I cannot tell: God knoweth;) how that he was caught up into paradise, and heard unspeakable words, which it is not lawful for a man to utter. Of such an one will I glory: yet of myself I will not glory, but in mine infirmities.

We are all interested in things having to do with a future life. We would like to know all we can about where people go immediately after death. And we would like to know, if possible, whether the dead are in a state of consciousness. And if so, are they aware of what we are doing here? It isn't mere curiosity every time. We will never be able to answer all the questions that come to our minds about death and dying, but that is probably a blessing. I am sure God loves us enough, if He felt we should know more, He would have told us more in the Scriptures. So we will content ourselves with what He has said in His word.

Physicians, psychologists, sociologists, and others have studied the subject in depth and have compiled some interesting information about "near death" experiences obtained from people who reportedly experienced something like the man of whom we read in II Corinthians 12:2, 4.

At first, some might think we would do well to quote some of those people or have a panel of physicians and psychologists who have treated them as patients who could comment "authoritatively" about such matters. Their patients could relate where they were, what they saw, and what they heard during their experiences. But on second thought, would that add authenticity to our study?

During our Lord's incarnation, He raised several people from the dead, people whom we know were dead. One was Jairus' daughter (Matthew 9). Another was the widow's son in the village of Nain (Luke 7). But the best known was Lazarus, many of the details of which are given us in John 11. We don't know how long the others had been dead. The widow's son's body was being carried in a casket to what seems might have been its burial when Jesus restored him to life. But Lazarus had been dead four days and his body had begun to deteriorate (verses 17, 39). Our Lord commanded him, "Lazarus come forth," and the dead man came forth from the grave and walked among his family and friends.

Now don't you suppose some of those friends who had comforted his sisters while Lazarus was dead and the multitudes who came to see him after he was raised were curious about where he was and what he knew during those four days? And don't you suppose they asked him some questions? I'm sure they did. But there's no such indication in the Scriptures.

And don't you know after the crowds had gone and Mary and Martha could talk with their brother in the quietness of their home, they would ask him, "Lazarus, where were you those four days? What did you see and hear? Did you know how we grieved over your death? Did you know about the funeral service we had for you? Did you know that Jesus came and wept with us?" Of course they did. But inspiration says nothing about it.

I have a good idea from what we learn from II Corinthians

12 that when Lazarus returned to his body, those things faded from his memory, and he couldn't have related them if he had wanted to. Paul said of himself,

> ... (whether in the body, I cannot tell: whether out of the body, I cannot tell: God knoweth:) such an one caught up into the third heaven, paradise, and heard unspeakable words, which it is not lawful for a man to utter.

If Paul was forbidden to report what he saw and heard, surely the widow's son was too, and Jairus' daughter, and Lazarus, and even those who may have had similar experiences in our generation. In fact, if one of them should tell us about it, we would question his integrity because of what the Scripture has revealed to us.

So what does the Bible say? Man is of dual nature. He is physical. His body is of the earth, earthy. His spirit is of God, spiritual. Paul declares: "While our outward man [the body] perishes, yet the inward man [the spirit] is renewed day by day" (II Corinthians 4:16). From Ecclesiastes 12:7, we learn at death the body returns to the earth from which God formed it in the beginning (Genesis 2:7) and the spirit returns to God who gave it (Zechariah 12:1). The Holy Spirit clearly divides the human being into flesh and spirit and declares the flesh came from one source and the spirit another when He says, "We have had fathers of our flesh which corrected us, and we gave them reverence; shall we not much rather be in subjection unto the father of spirits, and live" (Hebrews 12:9)?

Now we know what Jesus meant when He said to the penitent thief on the cross, "Today shalt thou be with me in paradise." Though they both would die that day, the spirit of each would continue on in Paradise. And a few verses later in that twenty-third chapter of Luke, Jesus cried with a loud voice and said, "Father, into thy hands I commend my spirit." Then He gave up the ghost (the spirit), his body became lifeless, and was taken by friends and buried.

In the seventh chapter of Acts we have the story of the

stoning of Stephen. As he died, he cried, "Lord, Jesus, receive my spirit" (verse 59). So people don't cease to exist at death. The body goes to the grave or to ashes, and the spirit lives on somewhere.

Does the spirit go immediately to its eternal destiny, to Heaven or to Hell? Perhaps you have heard preachers at the funeral of a loved one say something to the effect, "Your dear mother is right now in Heaven singing in the angels' choir." Well, I'm sorry, that is a mistake. In the first place, it isn't within him to say where Mother is. Funerals are not for the purpose of determining the destiny of the departed spirit or where the deceased will spend eternity. And next, the spirit doesn't go directly into Heaven, if by "Heaven" one means the eternal dwelling place of God. It goes, rather, to another place to await the judgment, then to the eternal abode.

Now let me tell you why I said that. The Bible teaches there is to be a general judgment when all men will be judged. We'll speak more fully to this subject in another message, but I must mention it here. You see, if people were judged at death and went immediately and directly to Heaven or Hell, there would be no purpose for the judgment. Jesus spoke of this judgment day as being universal in its scope. All nations—past, present and future—will be there He said (Matthew 25:31, 32). He also said, "The men of Nineveh shall rise in the judgment with this generation" (Matthew 12:41). And in the next verse, "The queen of the south shall rise up in the judgment with this generation." The men of Nineveh lived some five hundred years before Christ's day on earth, and the Queen of the South lived a thousand years before. Yet Jesus said they will be in the same judgment with the people of His generation.

And when Peter preached on the day of Pentecost, A.D. 33, he said, "David has not yet ascended into Heaven" (Acts 2:32). David, too, had been dead about a thousand years but Peter, by the inspiration of the Holy Spirit, said he had not yet ascended into Heaven. (A television viewer heard me say this; in anger she wrote me that she would never see another program of ours because she *knew* her dead mother was in Heaven. She knew she went there the day she died. Well, all right, but David and others mentioned in the Bible didn't.) And the Bible says, "The Lord knows how to deliver the godly out of temptations, and to reserve the unjust unto the day of judgment to be punished" (II Peter 2:9). So where are the Ninevites, the Queen of the South, David, the unjust, and all the others who have died and gone from among us? They are somewhere awaiting the same judgment in which you and I will appear. Well, where is that?

Are they in Purgatory? The Bible says nothing about Purgatory. Neither the word nor the doctrine is found in the Scriptures, so we'll not spend a lot of time on it. We will only examine it as a legitimate part of this study. Since it isn't a biblical doctrine, we turn to other literature to learn what we can about it. From the *Encyclopedia of Religion & Religions* and the *Encyclopedia Britannica*, we learn the idea was first conceived by Thomas Aquinas, thirteenth century theologian-philosopher. It became a part of Catholic doctrine at the Council of Trent (1545-1563). Simply and briefly stated, Purgatory is thought to be a state of suffering after death in which the souls of those who die in "venial sin," and of those who still owe some debt of temporal punishment for "mortal sin," are rendered fit to enter Heaven. But since the Bible says nothing about it, and since the Bible holds out no hope of another chance at salvation after death and before the judgment, we may be certain our departed loved ones are not there.

Are they in Hades? We often use the words *Hades* and *Hell* interchangeably, but they are not the same. *Hades* is the unseen world, the world of departed spirits. The word also means "all-receiving," as it receives every soul that departs life in this world, both the good and the bad. Even Christ went to Hades for those three days and nights His body rested in the tomb (Acts 2:27, 31). Unfortunately the King James version translates the word as *hell* in these verses, but the American Standard and other versions translate it *Hades*. So every person who dies, goes to Hades. *All* of our friends and loved ones who have died, have gone to, and are in Hades.

But Jesus promised the thief on the cross, "Today shalt thou be with me in paradise." Right? Then Paradise is that part—or shall we say state—of Hades to which the righteous go. But Paradise is not Heaven, if we mean by "Heaven" the dwelling place of God, the eternal abode of the righteous. Jesus spent those three days and nights in Paradise in Hades. But after He was resurrected He told Mary, "Touch me not, for I have not yet ascended to the Father" (John 20:17).

Paradise means "a pleasure garden." Yes, it is sometimes used with reference to Heaven, but that doesn't mean it must always mean Heaven. Heaven is also called a city, but that doesn't mean every city mentioned in the Scriptures is Heaven. The departed saved people are in Paradise, Hades awaiting the judgment, after which they will enter into Heaven for all eternity.

We mentioned a moment ago that God has "reserved the unjust unto the day of judgment to be punished" (II Peter 2:9). Well, where are they reserved? They are in Hades too, but they are in the place or state called Tartarus. In II Peter 2:4, Peter declares, "For God spared not the angels that sinned, but cast them down to Tartarus, and delivered them into chains of darkness, to be reserved unto judgment." Again, it is unfortunate the King James version translates *Tartarus* as "hell," but some Bibles have a marginal note, "Tartarus." Tartarus is in Hades, on the other side of "a fixed gulf" from Paradise and Heaven (Luke 16:19-31).

From II Peter 2:4, we know that is where all of the wicked, unforgiven people have gone to await the judgment. It is not Hell, the eternal abode of the unforgiven wicked dead. It is a prison where they are held in torment until judgment day. After the judgment, they will enter into Hell itself, where they will suffer eternally.

So my friend, our departed loved ones are in Hades. If they were saved by an obedient and trusting faith in Jesus Christ, they are in Paradise, Hades awaiting the judgment to go on into Heaven to live forever. If they died without Christ, they are in Tartarus, Hades, awaiting the day of judgment, and there is a great gulf fixed so they cannot cross over into Paradise and Heaven. They are fully conscious. The righteous are enjoying the pleasure garden of Paradise, and the unrighteous are imprisoned and are tormented there. None of them know what we are doing here on earth (Ecclesiastes 9:5). And if they did, it is very likely they would be like the rich man of Luke 16. They would want urgently to send us a message to be saved at once, without delay.

My friend, God has made every provision He can to prevent man from a life of punishment in the other world. However, in His righteous character, God must punish the wicked and disobedient as well as reward the righteous and the obedient. A person's eternal destiny is irrevocably determined by the time he dies. The Bible doesn't offer another chance. It says nothing of works of supererogation. In His story of the rich man and Lazarus in Luke 16, Jesus makes it clear that there is no crossing the great gulf to go from Paradise to Tartarus or from Tartarus to Paradise. So it is extremely urgent that we give attention to the important things while we may.

God bless you. I love you.

QUESTIONS FOR CLASS DISCUSSION

1. What are some of the things people would like to know about their deceased loved ones? To whom can we turn to know?

2. Name three people Christ raised from the dead and what they told about their experiences in the world of the dead.

3. How do you feel about people travelling around the country telling of their five or seven days in heaven or with God?

4. Discuss "Purgatory," "Hades," "Paradise."

5. What Scriptures did you learn from this study that strengthen your faith in life after death?

11

The Judgment

Hebrews 9:27

And as it is appointed unto men once to die, but after this the judgment.

Do you believe in a day of judgment for all people? Do you believe in justice, a balancing of the books, so to speak, of the injustices some of us have perpetrated against others? Do you believe in the justice of God? Or is He a God of love in whom there is no justice?

Judgment day! What a frightening thought for some people! Is that one of the fears you have of death and dying? It is with a lot of people. You are probably thinking this is one doctrine on which all professed Christians are agreed, but if you think that, you are mistaken. It isn't true.

It is taught by some believers that because God is the God of love, He will, in the finality of things, forgive all people and everyone will be saved without a judgment. Others are undecided about the exact nature of this final judgment.

Some think it means those who are lost will live on eternally conscious of their banishment from the presence of God. And others say, "No! It won't be that way," that such judgment means life eternal for the righteous but annihilation for the unrighteous. Some teach judgment and Hell are a dark reality,

- 83 -

but that these doctrines don't stand at the center of Jesus' teachings about human destiny. They believe God did not send his Son into the world to judge the world, but that the world through Him might be saved. So we ask, "What does the Bible say about a day of judgment?"

First, let's see what Jesus really did teach about judgment. In that familiar passage often called the golden text of the Bible (John 3:16), He said, "God so loved the world, that he gave his only begotten Son, that whosoever believeth in him should not perish, but have everlasting life." Then He continued, "For God sent not his Son into the world to condemn [or judge] the world; but that the world through him might be saved." The same thought is repeated in John 12:47 and other passages.

No one questions those precious passages. But it is an error to use them to deny either a day of judgment or that Christ shall judge the world. Look at what He said in John 5:22: "The Father judgeth no man, but hath committed all judgment unto the Son." And He continues in verse 26: "For as the Father hath life in himself; so hath he given to the Son to have life in himself; and hath given him authority to execute judgment also, because he is the Son of man." And even further in verse 30, He says, "I can of mine own self do nothing; as I hear, I judge; and my judgment is just because I seek not mine own will, but the will of the Father which hath sent me."

Does Jesus contradict Himself when in one set of passages He says He came not into the world to judge but to save, and in another set of passages He says God has given Him authority to judge? Of course not. He is simply saying when He came the first time, it was to save, not to judge, and when He returns, He will come to judge, not to save.

The truth of the matter is, the doctrine of judgment is very much at the center of our Savior's teachings about human destiny. He has so very much to say about judgment as it relates to our destiny. Read the gospels and underscore those passages having to do with the destiny of man. See if judgment is not essential, basic, and at the center of it. Don't take my word for it or anyone else's.

Judgment is certain! The Scripture says, "It is appointed unto men once to die, and after this the judgment" (Hebrews 9:27). We might say, then, that the judgment is as certain as death itself! And just as there is no escape from death, there is no escape from the judgment. By inspiration of the Holy Spirit, Paul wrote the Christians at Corinth, "We must all appear before the judgment seat of Christ" (II Corinthians 5:10). And on Mars Hill he preached,

> [God] now commandeth all men everywhere to repent; because he hath appointed a day, in the which he will judge the world in righteousness by that man whom he hath ordained; whereof he hath given assurance unto all men; in that he hath raised him from the dead (Acts 17:30, 31).

Need I say more? I could. But surely, there is no room for doubt about it. As certainly as we must die, we must all be judged.

When will judgment occur? Jesus said,

> When the Son of man shall come in his glory, and all the holy angels with him, then shall he sit upon the throne of his glory; and before him shall be gathered all nations; and he shall separate them one from another, as a shepherd divideth his sheep from the goats; and he shall set the sheep on his right hand, but the goats on the left. Then shall the King say unto them on his right hand, come, ye blessed of my father, inherit the kingdom prepared for you from the foundation of the world. . . . Then shall he say also unto them on the left hand, depart from me ye cursed, into everlasting fire, prepared for the devil and his angels. . . . And these shall go away into everlasting punishment; but the righteous into life eternal (Matthew 25:31-34, 41, 46).

Please notice it will be at the next appearing of our Lord that judgment and final separation of the righteous from the wicked will occur. It isn't something that has occurred already, or will occur at our death. When Christ comes again, that will be the end (I Corinthians 15:23, 24; II Peter 3:1-12). The heavens and the earth shall be burned up and all men will assemble before the judgment bar of the almighty and all-knowing God.

Who will be present? All nations from the beginning of time until the end will be present. The wicked and the righteous will be present at the same appearance and same judgment. Some teach there will be at least a thousand years between the judgment of the righteous and the unrighteous. But that isn't so. We will all appear there together. And the Lord will separate the one from the other, as a shepherd separates his sheep from the goats, the sheep on the right hand, and the goats on the left.

Paul the apostle declares,

> For we must all appear before the judgment seat of Christ; that every one may receive the things done in his body according to that he hath done, whether it be good or bad, knowing therefore the terror of the Lord, we persuade men (II Corinthians 5:10, 11).

So you will be there. And I will be there. And your neighbor will be there, and mine. This is one appointment we have with God not one of us will miss! Not a one!

Who will be the judge? There is a very interesting passage in I Corinthians 4:3-5. Paul speaks of his own stewardship:

> But with me it is a very small thing that I should be judged of you, or man's judgment; yea, I judge not mine own self. For I know nothing by myself; yet am I not hereby justified; but he that judgeth me is the Lord. Therefore judge nothing before the time, until the Lord come, who both will bring to light the hidden things of darkness, and will make manifest the counsels of the hearts; and then shall every man have praise of God.

Paul is simply saying we won't be judging one another. Isn't that great news? I don't want to sit in judgment on you. I have been called on for jury duty. Have you? I think it is a duty of our citizenship to serve when called upon to do so. I don't believe in trying to be excused, but I just have to admit, I don't like to do it. I do not like to sit in judgment on other people. I just don't. And I'm glad I am not going to be judged by some people I know, too! Let's face it, some folks are prejudiced. They don't get all the facts before they come up with a verdict. Some don't even want to know all the facts first. So we won't be judging one another, and I am glad of that. Aren't you?

But that comes as no surprise to you, does it? However, what Paul said next may come as a surprise. He said, "Yea, I judge not my own self. For I know nothing by myself [or against myself], but am I not hereby justified." So we will not be permitted to judge ourselves. Can't you imagine how that would turn out? Since I don't know anything against myself, I might just pass me on into Heaven. But it won't work that way. You see, we will be judged by One who knows everything, One who will bring to light the hidden things and reveal even the secrets of the heart. Say! that judgment is going be to thorough! And it will be final! There will be no appeals court. That will be it! Final! Eternal! Irrevocable!

Still another question is on the minds of some. On what basis will people be judged? As recorded in Revelation 20:11-15, John saw a vision of the judgment scene and wrote:

> I saw a great white throne, and him that sat on it, from whose face the earth and the heaven fled away; and there was found no place for them. And I saw the dead, small and great stand before God; and the books were opened: and another book was opened, which is the book of life: and the dead were judged out of those things which were written in the books according to their works. And the sea gave up the dead which were in it; and death and hell were cast into the lake of fire. This is the second death. And whosoever was not found written in the book of life was cast into the lake of fire.

First, the dead are judged out of the books which were opened. These are the law of God. Jesus once said, "He that rejecteth me, and receiveth not my words, hath one that judgeth him; the word that I have spoken, the same shall judge him in the last day" (John 12:48). So those books are the revelation of God's will to men. The patriarchs will be held accountable to the law which was given them; the Jews under Moses' law will be judged by that law; and we who live in the Christian age will be judged by the teachings of Christ.

One may object, "But I don't believe the Bible." My friend, you may not believe it, but you will be judged by it. It applies to you whether you accept it or not. The verse also says, "And they were judged every man according to their works." We must each one of us give account for our deeds, the deeds done in the body, whether they were good or bad (II Corinthians 5:10)—every one of us, individually, and personally. And verse 15 says, "And whosoever was not found written in the book of life was cast into the lake of fire." Right beside the books of the law of God will be another book called the Lamb's Book of Life. It will be open, and if one's name is not in it, he will be lost. Is your name in that book? That should be a matter of high priority with every one of us. Is yours there? It is if you have become a Christian and are living faithfully.

Like death, judgment cannot be avoided or escaped. You can't excuse yourself from it or be absent that day, but you can prepare for it. It isn't as some people seem to think: "If judgment isn't held in our church building, I won't attend." We will all be there whether we have believed in it or not. Now is the time to get ready for it. The old revival song so familiar to many people said,

> There's a great day coming;
> A great day coming;
> There's a great day coming by and by.

The second stanza said,

> There's a sad day coming;
> A sad day coming;
> There's a sad day coming by and by.

And the third stanza said,

> There's a glad day coming;
> A glad day coming;
> There's a glad day coming by and by.

It will be a great day, none like it ever. And whether it is sad or glad depends on the individual and his preparedness. If you are a Christian, it will be a glad event. If not, it will be a sad one. Repent and obey the Lord in baptism at once, my friend.

May the Lord bless you. I really do love you.

QUESTIONS FOR CLASS DISCUSSION

1. What did Jesus say about a judgment?
2. Who is to be the judge?
3. Who will be in the judgment? Name some the Bible mentions.
4. Discuss the practice of revivalists of using judgment as a motivation to repentance.
5. Will judgment day be a great day or a sad day?

12

Heaven

Revelation 21:1, 2, 10, 11, 17-21

And I saw a new heaven and a new earth: for the first heaven and the first earth were passed away; and there was no more sea. And I John saw the holy city, new Jerusalem, coming down from God out of heaven, prepared as a bride adorned for her husband. . . . And he carried me away in the spirit to a great and high mountain, and shewed me that great city, the holy Jerusalem, descending out of heaven from God. . . . And he measured the wall thereof, an hundred and forty and four cubits, according to the measure of a man, that is, of the angel. And the building of the wall of it was of jasper: and the city was pure gold, like unto clear glass. And the foundations of the wall of the city were garnished with all manner of precious stones. The first foundation was jasper; the second, sapphire; the third, a chalcedony; the fourth, an emerald; the fifth, sardonyx; the sixth, sardius; the seventh, chrysolyte; the eighth, beryl; the ninth, a topaz; the tenth, a chrysoprasus; the eleventh, a jacinth; the twelfth, an amethyst. And the twelve gates were twelve pearls: every several gate was of one pearl: and the street of the city was pure gold, as it were transparent glass.

In his book, *Adventures In Immortality,* Dr. George Gallup wrote that seventy-one percent of us in America believe in Heaven, and that that percentage has held steady for the past thirty years. When Gallup asked believers, "Where is Heaven?" someone replied, "Up there." Another said, "Another dimension." Still another responded, "It's not Brooklyn." And someone else said, "I have no earthly idea." Well, what about it?

The word *heaven* appears literally hundreds of times in the

Bible—582 times to be exact, 327 times in the Old Testament and 255 times in the New. If a person believes the Bible and respects its teachings, he believes in Heaven. Any preaching or system of teaching that denies the hope of Heaven, denies the credibility of the Bible and reduces man to the level of the beasts of the earth and the birds of the heavens. Still occasionally we hear someone preaching or teaching that whatever Heaven there is, is what we make for ourselves right here on the earth.

Where is Heaven? Well, we can agree with the lady from Brooklyn—it isn't there! It isn't here on the earth anywhere! Heaven is not a state or condition which we find or achieve here in this life. It is a real place, just as real as if it were in Brooklyn or some spot in Texas. Neither is it "another dimension." Heaven is not "a fantasy," "a state of mind," or an "invention of the clergy." It is a place, a real place! Jesus said, "I go to prepare a *place* for you. And if I go and prepare a place for you, I will come again, and receive you unto myself; that where I am, there ye may be also" (John 14:1-3). The apostle Peter spoke of the Christian's inheritance in I Peter 1:3, 4. He said,

> Blessed be the God and Father of our Lord Jesus Christ, which according to his abundant mercy hath begotten us again unto a lively [living] hope by the resurrection of Jesus Christ from the dead, to an inheritance incorruptible, and undefiled, and that fadeth not away, reserved in heaven for you.

Where is our inheritance? It is in Heaven. Despite the fact that we can neither see it nor touch it nor smell nor taste nor hear it; it is real. For, "we look not at the things which are seen, but at the things which are not seen; for the things which are seen are temporal; but the things which are not seen are eternal" (II Corinthians 4:18).

In II Corinthians 12:2 the apostle Paul wrote, "I knew a man in Christ above fourteen years ago (whether in the body, I cannot tell; or whether out of the body, I cannot tell; God knoweth); such an one caught up to the third heaven," which indicates that insofar as Scripture is concerned there are at least three heavens.

The first is the atmosphere immediately above the surface of and surrounding the earth in which the birds fly and the clouds gather. The Bible speaks of the "fowl of heaven" (Genesis 7:23).

The second heaven is above that one and is what we commonly call "outer space." It is where the sun, the moon, the stars and the planets are. David said, "The heavens declare the glory of God, and the firmament showeth his handiwork" (Psalm 19:1). We are learning more and more about this vast area of our universe, and the more we learn of it, the more the heavens declare the glory of God.

The third heaven is the eternal dwelling place of God (Isaiah 66:1). It is up above the others whence the Son of God came to dwell among us as a man (John 3:13). "He that descended is the same also that ascended up far above all heavens, that he might fill all things" (Ephesians 4:10). It is also the eternal dwelling place of the saints (II Corinthians 5:1). No one, I repeat, no one has ever gone into the third heaven—to the Paradise of God—and returned to tell what he saw and heard. If you have been having any business dealings with someone who says he has been there for four or five days, you had better start counting your change. If the Bible is true, he is not! The apostle Paul went there, but was not permitted to tell what he saw and heard (II Corinthians 12:1-4). The apostle John was given a vision of it on the Isle of Patmos but was not actually there. So don't you be deceived by these people going about the country with false claims of special visits to Heaven and privileges with God.

What is Heaven like? Well, since no one has ever gone there and returned to tell us about it, it must be obvious that we are dependent on the word of God to know what we can. Is it really a city fifteen hundred miles long, fifteen hundred miles wide, and fifteen hundred miles high, made of pure gold like clear glass? And is it really surrounded by a wall of jasper seventy-two yards wide? And does it actually have twelve gates each made of real pearl and streets of pure gold like transparent glass? And are the foundations made of every kind of precious stone: jasper and sapphire and chalcedony; emerald and sardonyx; sardius and chrysolite and beryl and topaz and chrysoprasus; and jacinth and amethyst? And does it actually have a beautiful river right down the middle of the street, flowing with the water of life, as clear as crystal?

This is part of the description of Heaven as we read it awhile ago from Revelation (chapter 21). But surely no one thinks that this place of spiritual existence and spiritual beauty is going to be that materialistic. When we say that, someone is ready to question our faith in the word of God. But we all know that Revelation is a book of signs and symbols (1:1). And surely God must be giving us a description of the eternal home of the soul in the only terms which we are capable of grasping. Oh! I have absolutely no doubt about it, my friend, Heaven is going to be a place of far greater beauty and magnificence and glory than can possibly be conveyed in those terms of physical beauty. If God had tried to describe to us the beauty of Heaven in terms which are purely spiritual, we could never have comprehended it at all. So He used terms with which we are all familiar and painted a word picture of the most beautiful setting our earthly minds could grasp.

When we returned from living in Australia, people often asked us, "What's it like there?" We could only tell them in terms of some city or place with which they were familiar here in America. Without such a comparison, they could never have understood what we were saying. But when we would say, "The climate in the city of Perth is like that of San Diego, California," or "the people are much like the people of Oklahoma City"; then they understood. Be assured, Heaven will be all of what you read in Revelation 21 and 22, and more! And more! *And more!*

What excites me about Heaven is that it is my eternal home!

I'll no longer be a stranger and a foreigner and a sojourner. I'll be at home with my heavenly Father, and with my older brother Jesus Christ, and with all of the redeemed souls of all ages. What is important to me is that there shall not enter into Heaven anything that is unclean or that makes an abomination or a lie (Revelation 21:8). The fearful and unbelieving and abominable and murderers and whoremongers and sorcerers and idolaters and all liars will be turned away (Revelation 21:8). And those whose garments have been made white in the blood of the lamb of God slain at Calvary will be citizens there.

I am thrilled over the fact that there will be no sickness, and suffering, and dying over there. People whose lives have been literally filled with pain and sorrow have every right to long for a place where there will be none. People who have had what seems to be more than their fair share of tragedy and dying and disappointment have a legitimate reason to look forward to Heaven where there will be no more of it. Call it pie-in-the-sky religion if you like. I believe in it and I am not ashamed to say it. There just has to be a place for those people to rest from all of that. Say, my friend, don't you want to go there?

There is another question I have been asked by many viewers: "Will we know each other in Heaven?" Every parent who has buried a child, every person who has had to give up a husband or wife or mother or father—someone who was especially dear—asks this question. I believe the Bible teaches that we will retain our identity and our personality by which we will be identified in the life beyond. We will not be recognized by our bodies because that isn't always possible even here in this life. Quite often when I am out over the country preaching, which I do every week—I am at a different church almost every Sunday—someone will come rushing up to me and say, "Do you remember me? I was a little girl when you knew me." Or, "You are the first preacher I remember when I was a child." Of course, I don't recognize them! Their bodies have changed so that I couldn't be expected to know them. Would I recognize them by their bodies in Heaven? No, not any more than I do here, but our personalities, whatever that is, are not dependent on our physical organisms.

The Bible says that when Abraham, Isaac, and Jacob died, they were "gathered to their people" (Genesis 25:8; 35:39; 49:33). David believed he would see his child who died at birth. He said, "He is dead, wherefore should I fast? Can I bring him back? I shall go to him, but he shall not return to me" (II Samuel 12:23). The apostles recognized Moses and Elijah on the mount of transfiguration (Matthew 17:1-5). So there is every reason to believe that we will know one another in Heaven. Heaven would not mean much if it were not true, if we did not remember past events and associations, if we were total strangers, non-entities there.

But that brings up another question: How can I be happy in Heaven if I am conscious and aware that some close relative or neighbor or friend or business associate is not in Heaven, but in Hell? I don't really know. But let me ask you this question: Are you happy now? Does the fact that this close relative or neighbor or friend or business associate is unsaved trouble you now so that you can't sleep at night or that you can't enjoy life here in this world? If it doesn't disturb your happiness or your routine here, it isn't likely it will there.

I have but one answer to all of the unknowns. It is my faith in an infinite God. If you grant me that premise, I have the key that unlocks the door of mystery to the things of the spirit for which there is no other key. Yes, while some are in Heaven others will be in Hell, and the sincere Christian will regret the loss of just one person in Hell. Yet somehow God has promised eternal happiness there, and I believe Him.

My friend, I don't want to miss Heaven. I hope to go there. I want more than anything else in all the world to be in Heaven. That is the ultimate goal of my life. How about you? Don't you want to go there too?

A certain father had a son who was nearing the age that he would be leaving home and going out on his own, so he thought it was time to have a father-son talk.

"Son," he asked, "what are your complete plans for the future?"

"You mean my whole life?"

"Yes."

"Well," the son replied after thinking it over, "when I get my degree, I am going to take that engineering job I've been offered."

"Good. What then?"

"Then Sue and I will get married as soon as we can."

"Fine, Sue is a splendid girl. What then?"

"If all goes well, I should get a promotion the first of the year, and more money, and we'll buy a house in that new section out by the lake."

"And what then?" the father asked.

"Well, I am sure we'll want at least two children."

The father smiled, "And what then?"

"I figure we'll need to set up a fund for the children's education. By then we should be set up to afford a trip around the world that I have always wanted."

"Sounds exciting. What then?"

"I am hoping they'll offer me a partnership in the company."

"And after that?"

"I guess that is about it. If I can do all these things, I figure I will just about have it made. We'll settle back and enjoy our grandchildren."

"But what then?" the father insisted.

"What do you mean, Dad? That will be it. Everything. What more could you ask for?"

"Well, son, if your hopes and dreams materialize strictly along those lines, you'll have missed the greatest blessing of all."

The son was puzzled, taken back. "Son, if you miss Heaven, you will have missed it all."

My friend, is Heaven in your plans? Be saved today, washed

in the blood of Jesus as you are baptized into His death (Romans 6:3). Will you?

God bless you. I love you.

QUESTIONS FOR CLASS DISCUSSION

1. Does anybody believe in Heaven anymore? Does anybody think there is a possibility of their going to Heaven?

2. Is Heaven a place? If so, where is it?

3. Examine John's description of Heaven in Revelation 21. Is that to be taken literally? Explain.

4. How will we know one another in Heaven?

5. What thought about Heaven excites you most?

13

Hell

Mark 9:43-47

And if thy hand offend thee, cut it off: it is better for thee to enter into life maimed, than having two hands to go into hell, into the fire that never shall be quenched: where their worm dieth not, and the fire is not quenched. And if thy foot offend thee, cut it off: it is better for thee to enter halt into life, than having two feet to be cast into hell, into the fire that never shall be quenched: where their worm dieth not, and the fire is not quenched. And if thine eye offend thee, pluck it out: it is better for thee to enter into the kingdom of God with one eye, than having two eyes to be cast into hell fire.

This series of messages was prompted by frequent requests from viewers of our television program, *In Search of the Lord's Way,* some of whom had suffered the loss of loved ones and had questions about their whereabouts and consciousness. Others were interested in some "near death" experiences of which there is so much talk. Others were disturbed by these people who are going through the country claiming to have spent several days in Heaven and returned with a message from God. And still others had an interest in the subject aroused by some of the current books and magazine articles on death and dying. There were more requests for copies of these programs than any we had ever done, to this time so perhaps we have been some encouragement to people when they needed it. If so, we are grateful.

The general attitude about Hell right now is that it should be written off as a relic of the superstitious past along with ghosts and goblins and such like. Current religious thought is, "Prophesy not unto us right things, speak unto us smooth things, prophesy deceits" (Isaiah 30:10). Consequently most of the preaching these days stresses being positive, and Hell is not very positive. So we are hearing a lot of preaching about goodness and love and forgiveness and joy—and there is a place for all of that. Don't misunderstand me, I love to preach about those things myself. But how long has it been since you heard a sermon about Hell in the church where you worship? Some denominations have rejected the biblical teaching about Hell altogether.

If we can put any confidence in the teachings of Jesus (and I can), it is a tragic and lamentable fact that the vast majority of people now living will go to Hell. He said,

> Enter ye in at the strait gate. For wide is the gate, and broad is the way, that leadeth to destruction, and many there be which go in thereat; because strait is the gate and narrow is the way which leadeth unto life, and few there be that find it (Matthew 7:13, 14).

Yes, the great masses of people jammed and crowded into the broad way are doomed to be lost in Hell. Many of them prefer not to be disturbed about it. And most popular professional preachers placate them.

Some people feel that the idea of Hell is born of revenge and brutality, but it isn't so. The idea is born of God and God is love. But how does one reconcile a place of intense suffering with the love of God? Well, let's let God speak for Himself in His word.

In the Old Testament, *hell* is the word generally and unfortunately used by our translators to render the Hebrew word *Sheol*. But *Sheol* really means the unseen world, the abode of the departed souls awaiting the judgment day, without consideration of their eternal destiny. It is true that in many passages *Sheol* can only mean the grave—such as in Genesis 37:35, in which Jacob, having heard of the alleged death of Joseph, cried out in his grief, "I will go down into the grave [*Sheol*] unto my son mourning." In other passages it is clearly the abode of the departed spirits at death, as in Psalm 16:10.

In the New Testament, *hell* appears as the translation of three words: *Hades* which is the Greek equivalent of *Sheol* meaning the place of the departed spirits; *Tartarus* which is found only in II Peter 2:4 and refers to the place where the wicked are imprisoned awaiting the day of final judgment, and *Gehenna* which appears most often and refers to the place of eternal punishment of the wicked. Gehenna is Hell!

Gehenna first referred to the Valley of Hinnom which is a deep and narrow valley to the south and west of Jerusalem. The first mention of it in the Bible is in Joshua 15:8 and 18:16 where it is established as the boundary line between the tribes of Judah and Benjamin. It was in the Valley of Hinnom that Solomon erected high places for Molech (I Kings 16:3; II Chronicles 28:3; 33:6). So by the time of our Lord, the Valley of Hinnom was a place of historical shame to the people of God.

To add to all of the moral and spiritual pollution, this valley became the garbage dump and the sewage disposal for the city. It burned day and night and the terrible stench of it was blown by the winds across the city. The fires never went out. Bodies of dead animals and criminals were thrown there and the place crawled constantly with worms. This was the Valley of Hinnom—Gehenna.

I am not saying that this is the Hell that awaits the unrighteous and ungodly after judgment. There are sects and cults who so teach. But what I am saying is that Jesus was describing the eternal destiny of the wicked in terms that the mind of man could grasp. He used the word *Gehenna* 'Hell' to say it is a place of moral and spiritual corruption, a place of shame and every kind of filth conceivable.

And He must have been trying to tell us that Hell is a place like that, only a thousand times worse. Just as we observed in the preceding chapter, that language is inadequate to describe the beauties, the grandeurs, and the glories of Heaven, so it is equally as inadequate in describing the filth, the stench, and the miseries of Hell. So as He did in the description of Heaven, Jesus does in the description of Hell, He speaks of something people could understand here in this world.

Oddly enough, in view of current religious thought pertaining to the subject, Jesus spoke of Hell more than any other person in the New Testament. The word *Gehenna* is used twelve times in the New Testament and it is used eleven of those twelve times by our Lord Himself.

In Matthew 5:22 He said,

> I say unto you, that whosoever is angry with his brother without a cause shall be in danger of the judgment; and whosoever shall say to his brother, Raca, shall be in danger of the council; but whosoever shall say, thou fool, shall be in dander of hell fire.

In Matthew 5:29 and the corresponding passage which we chose for the scripture text earlier from Mark, He said,

> And if thy hand offend thee, cut it off; it is better for thee to enter into life maimed, than having two hands to go into hell, into the fire that never shall be quenched; where the worm dieth not, and the fire is not quenched. And if thy foot offend thee, cut it off; it is better for thee to enter halt into life, than having two feet to be cast into hell, into the fire that never shall be quenched; where the worm dieth not and the fire is not quenched. And if thine eye offend thee, pluck it out; it is better for thee to enter into the kingdom of God with one eye, than having two eyes to be cast into hell fire; where the worm dieth not, and the fire is not quenched.

In Matthew 10:28 when He sent the Twelve out on the limited commission, He charged them, "Fear not them which kill the body, but are not able to kill the soul; but rather fear him which is able to destroy both soul and body in hell."

Jesus used other terms to describe Hell. He spoke of the separation from Him as "the light of the world" as being cast into "outer darkness" (Matthew 8:12). He emphasized the indescribable agonies there by saying, "There shall be weeping and gnashing of teeth" (Matthew 8:12). He said in Hell "the fire is not quenched."

Did Jesus believe in Hell? Oh! Yes He did! In fact no one in the Bible spoke more definitely on the subject than He. As we said before, other than one reference found in James 3:6, Jesus is the only one to use the term at all in the New Testament. He described it in the strongest way possible. I am saying that our Lord is to be taken seriously on this subject. Yet, it is not to be taken that God receives any pleasure in the thought of Hell. He has said,

> As I live, saith the Lord God, I have no pleasure in the death of the wicked; but that the wicked turn from his way and live; turn ye, turn ye from your evil ways; for why will ye die (Ezekiel 23:11)?

It is important for us to know who will be in hell. Since we cannot pass judgment on other people, we must leave that to the Lord, too. What does He say in His word?

In Revelation 20:12-15, we are given a vision of the judgment. John wrote,

> And I saw the dead, small and great, stand before God; and the books were opened: and another book was opened, which is the book of life: and the dead were judged out of those things which were written in the books, according to their works. And the sea gave up the dead which were in it; and death and hell delivered up the dead which were in them: and they were judged every man according to their works. And death and hell were cast into the lake of fire. This is the second death. And whosoever was not found written in the book of life was cast into the lake of fire.

And in Revelation 21:8 He said,

> The fearful, and unbelieving and the abominable, and murderers, and whoremongers, and sorcerers, and idolaters, and all liars, shall have their part in the lake which

burneth with fire and brimstone; which is the second death.

From this you can see that Hell is not only going to be a place of spiritual darkness and corruption, a place of weeping and gnashing of teeth, but it will be the dumping ground for all moral and spiritual filth. I have heard people say, "I don't go to church because there are too many hypocrites there." But let me tell you something, my friend and brother: I would much, much rather be in church with a hypocrite for a few hours here on earth than to have to live for all eternity with that crowd in Hell! Now, wouldn't you?

Can a loving God send anyone to Hell? Many of us have created a mental image of God that would not permit anyone to go to hell for eternity. We just sort of believe that someway, somehow, God is going to come up with some last-minute scheme by which all of us will be saved in Heaven. He just will not permit anyone to be lost in Hell. If that is your image of God, you need to carve on it some. God does not want anyone to go to Hell. He loves us so much that He sent His only begotten Son to die on the cross to deliver us all from such a destiny. "He is longsuffering toward us, not willing that any should perish, but that all should come to repentance" (II Peter 3:9). He wants all men "to be saved and come to a knowledge of the truth" (I Timothy 2:4). Should any of us go to Hell, it will be contrary to God's will. His will is for us to be saved from it. So if we go there, it will be our own doing in spite of His will and his efforts to prevent it.

You must be a Christian, my friend. If you are to escape such a dreaded place, you must be a Christian. There is no other way. If there had been any other way, or if there were no Hell, Christ would not have had to die on the cross. If you could have done enough good works to be saved, He would not have had to be crucified. If you could have been sincere enough to be saved, Christ would not have had to shed His blood for you.

You determine your eternal destiny by the decision you make about Christ here in this life. To decide against Christ is